What Every Postdoc Needs to Know

What Every Postdoc Needs to Know

Liz Elvidge
Imperial College London, UK

Carol Spencely
University of Surrey, UK

Emma Williams
EJW Solutions Ltd, UK

World Scientific

NEW JERSEY · LONDON · SINGAPORE · BEIJING · SHANGHAI · HONG KONG · TAIPEI · CHENNAI · TOKYO

Published by

World Scientific Publishing Europe Ltd.

57 Shelton Street, Covent Garden, London WC2H 9HE

Head office: 5 Toh Tuck Link, Singapore 596224

USA office: 27 Warren Street, Suite 401-402, Hackensack, NJ 07601

Library of Congress Cataloging-in-Publication Data
Names: Elvidge, Liz, author. | Spencely, Carol, author. | Williams, Emma, author.
Title: What every Postdoc needs to know / by (author): Liz Elvidge (Imperial College London, UK),
    Carol Spencely (University of Surrey, UK), Emma Williams (EJW Solutions Ltd, UK).
Description: New Jersey : World Scientific, [2017]
Identifiers: LCCN 2016045896| ISBN 9781786342348 (hc : alk. paper) |
    ISBN 9781786342355 (pbk : alk. paper)
Subjects: LCSH: Doctoral students--Great Britain--Handbooks, manuals, etc.
Classification: LCC LB2386 .E58 2017 | DDC 378.2--dc23
LC record available at https://lccn.loc.gov/2016045896

British Library Cataloguing-in-Publication Data
A catalogue record for this book is available from the British Library.

Desk Editors: Dipasri Sardar/Mary Simpson/Shi Ying Koe

Typeset by Stallion Press
Email: enquiries@stallionpress.com

Printed in Singapore by B & Jo Enterprise Pte Ltd

Foreword

Being a Postdoc is not easy. When I look back at my own academic career, the 4 years I spent as a postdoc were by far the most challenging. I loved the research I was doing, but I had a young family, a long list of bills to pay each month, and no long-term career prospects.

It is a time of transition, as you leave your student years behind and embark on the fledgling steps towards either an academic career or, increasingly these days, the wider world of work. It is also a time of great uncertainty, with fixed-term contracts, when money can be short and where — after the exhilaration of finishing your PhD — work can suddenly seem quite mundane and repetitive, and doubts can start to creep in about your chosen path.

But there has been progress in recent years. An increasing appreciation of the enormous value of postdocs to university research, combined with an increasing awareness of the need for specialised support and advice, has led to a marked improvement in the environment in which postdocs live and work. Gone are the days in which postdocs were the forgotten "lab monkeys" exploited as a cheap and disposable resource.

Improving support for university postdocs has been a personal passion of mine for a long time. Over the 30 years when I was active in research I had the pleasure and privilege of working with more than 50 postdocs, incredibly talented young men and women from whom I learned so much and whose subsequent career development was a source of great pride. When I arrived at Imperial College London in 2013, I was therefore delighted to discover an institution that takes the support and development of its postdoc community very seriously, and whose Postdoc Development Centre is, I believe, an exemplar in the sector.

Imperial's Postdoc Development Centre offers a range of advice and services specially tailored to the needs of our more than 2,400 strong postdoc community. From career advice and CV workshops to networking opportunities and "family friendly" initiatives, the Centre is an exceptional resource. Its success is due in no small measure to the outstanding and inspirational leadership of its Director, Dr Liz Elvidge. Liz is a vocal and effective champion of postdocs, both here at Imperial and nationally. By working "hands-on" with the postdoc community, and especially by listening not only to their concerns, but also to their hopes and aspirations, she has been able to establish a robust and very effective support structure.

The success of the Postdoc Development Centre is due in no small part to the following people, co-authors of this book.

Dr Carol Spencely was the Centre's first Consultant. She effortlessly made the transition from postdoc to researcher developer at Imperial. She combines her expert knowledge, having been a postdoc at Imperial in Immunology, with the experience of balancing the demands of research, shifting careers and a love of working within higher education (HE).

Dr Emma Williams has been an external consultant for the Postdoc Development Centre since its inception. She brings both academic credibility from her previous work at Cambridge University with a flair for creativity in researcher development and an approachable style which makes her advice easily accessible from across all the disciplines.

Nowadays Liz, Carol and Emma are in great demand to visit other institutions and share the insights and good practice that has been developed here at Imperial. I am therefore delighted that they are now able to pass on their knowledge and experience to a much wider audience through this important book. It is not only the perfect "user guide" for any current or aspiring postdoc, but it should also, I believe, be required reading for those academics with postdoc management responsibilities.

Professor **James Stirling**, CBE, FRS, FInstP
Provost, Imperial College London.

Acknowledgements

This book was born because Laurent from the publishers asked Liz to write it. She contacted Emma and Carol and said …

I've been approached by a publisher to write a book for postdocs — something practical the postdocs could benefit from and he encouraged me to approach a couple of co-authors... Off the top of my head I've come up with these chapter titles so wondered whether you'd be interested? I wasn't sure when I met him but then the thought of the 3 of us working together would be a blast! We can do this!

So the buck stops there!

The authors are very grateful to our many kind reviewers who have helped us through this process. They have worked with typo ridden drafts and taken the time to suggest edits on all levels from the typographical to the philosophical. They have also provided much needed encouragement. So we profoundly thank Elizabeth Adams, Donald Beaton, Bill Dunn, Nigel Eady, Jo Montgomery Grindod, James Harker, Kathy Kingstone, Susie Maidment, Sharon Neal, Robert Nyman, Karina Prasad and John Woodward.

We would like to extend our thanks to those postdocs and academics who let us quote them in the text. Some have chosen to be anonymous — thank you, you know who you are. Thanks also to Marcela Acuña-Rivera, Nicola Ayers, Jessica Guennewich, Sam Hopkins, Alma López-Avilés, Ali Mobasheri, Bob Patton, Ivana Poparic and James Suckling.

We are particularly grateful to Professor James Stirling, CBE, FRS, FInstP, Provost of Imperial College London who agreed to write the Foreword. His continued support and championing of all things for postdocs is much appreciated and has made a real difference to the lives of many postdocs at Imperial.

Our cartoons were drawn by Mike Castillo and we are grateful for the revisions and patience as we tried to articulate ideas into pictures.

We are also grateful to our families and colleagues who have lived with us whilst we have been on this book writing journey. Apparently it has been a process best viewed behind a shield whilst proffering coffee.

This book would not have been possible without the many hundreds (thousands?) of academics, postdocs and graduate students we have worked with over the years whilst in research and supporting researchers.

What every postdoc needs to know about ... our supporters

- ☑ These fabulous people gave up their time to help us help you.
- ☑ We certainly owe these people a drink of their choice!
- ☑ You need people like them to give you feedback — start building your network!

Contents

Introduction

Why did we write this book?

In short, we want to help. Being a postdoc is a pivotal career stage and we want to make your journey easier. This book will tell you things that most people find out *during* their first postdoc contract, so you can stand on the shoulders of those who have gone before you. You can learn from the successes (and failures) of previous postdocs whom we have had the privilege of working with.

We want you to use your postdoc as a launchpad for a brilliant career. Please be aware that we do not have an agenda to drive you all towards industry, teaching or a lectureship; but we do have one simple rule:

A postdoc is not a career

Use your time as a contract researcher to build skills, gain experiences and develop an amazing CV so that you can move on to *your* choice of future. Please note, there is no magic-quick-fix-formula for achieving that amazing CV (if there was, we would sell it and be rich!); but, this book will guide you through the key things we feel you need to consider as a postdoc, and help to make you aware of those things you don't know you don't know.

What do we know?

We have all been there and worn the lab coat! We have then moved on from being postdocs to working in universities where our work has brought us directly into contact with the development needs and career concerns of postdocs. Alas, we haven't kept count of all the postdocs we have worked with but it must be, between the three of us, thousands. We have also worked with funders, University senior staff, national bodies and a range of employers who are keen for postdocs to understand the realities of postdoc life.

In addition to our golden rule (a postdoc is not a career), a prompt that we have found to help with a lot of researcher-related choices are the 3Ps: person, project, place. The 3Ps are referred to throughout this book and can help to clarify your thinking in a number of situations; e.g. when choosing where to do a postdoc you can think about your personal situation, the project, and the research environment. Taking opportunities — you can think about personal development, project-related opportunities, and what your institution has to offer. You can even apply it to teaching: person — what are you going to get out of taking on teaching; project — what will this particular teaching load involve — designing sessions, assessment, lectures, or practical sessions; place — who will you be working with, will you be part of the teaching committee, will you get feedback scores from students … The 3Ps really help with emphasising the personal development aspect of being a postdoc (person) which is an element that often gets overshadowed when thinking about the research work (project), and the environment that you are working in (place).

How to use this book

This is a work book, so grab a notebook to jot down your thoughts as you go along. As we have said above, the contents should help you get ahead by learning from other postdocs' experiences but there are no magic answers (sorry). There is plenty of advice, information and prompting for you to jump into action.

We have tried to arrange this book in a chronological order, starting from choosing a postdoc through to interviewing for your next position, but each chapter should stand alone. So, if you are feeling stressed dive into Chapter 11 or if you have a conference coming up then Chapter 9 has networking advice.

The examples and experiences we use in this book are mainly from the sciences because this is where our main expertise lies, but we have also worked with researchers from a wide range of disciplines (including history, dance, law, tourism, creative writing), and the key messages are the same. Our wish for this book is that it should become well-thumbed and passed around the postdocs and PhD students of a lab (unless of course you would all like to buy your own copy!) We apologize in advance for our sense of humour (which we realize is not appreciated by all, but which we hope will be tolerated for the useful content) but you do need to appreciate that we are British and our humour can be quite dry — unlike the weather!

What every postdoc needs to know about ... this book

We have formatted this book with the following symbols to make it clear what you should do at each stage:

☑ Something positive you should have/look into.
☒ Something negative you should avoid/bear in mind.
☐ A checklist for you to work through.

∗ Time for you to stop and think. Recording your answers in a notebook or electronically will help you clarify your thinking. Writing it down is key — to see your thoughts in black and white is very helpful.

At the end of each chapter you will find our three top tips and a list of further resources.

Chapter 1

Choosing a Postdoc

Do you really need to do a(nother) postdoc?

You have worked hard at academic study all your life through high school, undergraduate and possibly masters level degrees, and you are now entering the final throes of your PhD. The postdoc is the next obvious step, but is it the right one? It can be surprisingly easy to drift into being a postdoc but you need to consider the end game. Where do you hope to be in 5 years' time? You may not have a firm idea yet; however, if you do and are planning to join the family business then there may be better ways to add to your CV. If you are considering another postdoc, then read on!

A postdoc is a job and is not a continuation of your student status. It is a research role combined with training in the professional skills needed to be a researcher. It is true that some Principal Investigators (PIs) might still insist on being called your supervisor, but they are now your manager. A postdoc is the space in which you build your CV for the future — stacking it with papers, grant contributions and teaching experience so that you can meaningfully apply for fellowships, lectureships and beyond. It is also a first step on the employment ladder for many, and prior job experience (rather than just your student experience) may be important to some future employers. The table below summarises when it might be useful to have been a postdoc (adapted from Ryan Wheeler, Manager, Career & Postdoctoral Services, TSRI).

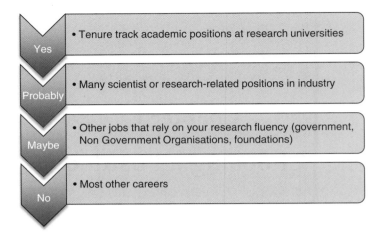

Not all career routes require postdoc experience

It should be noted that very few successful PhD candidates make it to "tenure track." According to The Royal Society report "The Scientific Century: securing our prosperity" only around 3.5% of PhD holders in Science Technology Engineering Maths (STEM) subjects make it to permanent academic research positions (lecturers and beyond). The majority enter the exciting array of "other" employment sectors.

> ## Postdoc drift
> The act of moving from PhD to postdoc as an automatic, natural next step without realising this is a real and pivotal career moment.

Current postdocs who were asked about why they chose to do a postdoc commented:

- "Just the necessary step and next step after a PhD."
- "I thought that's the pathway I'm supposed to take and I have to take."
- "For me, I just sort of rolled into it. It hasn't been like a career choice with a capital 'C'"
- "Natural progression from a PhD."

All at sea? Don't succumb to postdoc drift.

There are many benefits of being a postdoc. Your time as a postdoc can give you the opportunity to:

☑ work with new people, and build networks and collaborations,
☑ enhance your research skills,
☑ experience academic life as a member of staff,
☑ take on further responsibilities (teaching, supervision, grant writing),
☑ enhance your transferable skills (see the chapter on skills),
☑ build up a body of evidence for the next academic stage.

However, undertaking a postdoc does need to be a conscious and considered decision. For someone with a PhD there are many job options but often the sheltered cosiness of academic research calls: we know it, we know the rules. We may moan about it but we know how it operates so it seems easier to stay within this world than to venture into untested territory.

Moving out from the academic world after a lifetime of schooling, degrees and academic endeavour can be viewed as:

• challenging,
• exciting,
• terrifying,
• a betrayal of all that has been invested in you,

- a sense of failure that you did not make the grade (also see imposter syndrome),
- "giving up after all that training" and with a sense of bewilderment by family and friends,
- "getting a 'proper' job at last" by friends and family.

Society needs intelligent, numerate, literate people capable of independent problem solving in many areas of work, so it is important to study your options at the end of your PhD. It is obviously a fraught time of writing up and finishing off your research, but time must be made to plan your next career move. Take time to see what employment options are open to someone with your skill set. Many corporate graduate roles may still be open to you. Technical firms may view the PhD as a bonus and for others you may need to translate what having a PhD really means in terms of your suitability for a role — see exploring careers outside academia later in this book. As a student you will still have access to your institution's career service, use this to help you explore options to make sure that you are making an active decision to undertake a postdoc position and are not succumbing to postdoc drift.

We are not trying to put you off! But just so you are under no illusions, please note:

A postdoc is not a career

It is a stepping stone to the next stage in your career, which could be within academia or in other sectors. If staying in academic life, the next stage may be a personal fellowship, teaching post or a lecturing post. If planning to move on after your postdoc, the world could be your oyster with the right set of skills and experiences useful to employers in general (known as transferable skills). It is common for researchers to undertake a second postdoc contract, but this should only be considered if it adds something to your CV that the first did not (new skills, further publications). A chain of postdoc positions may give you employment for several years but these will be overshadowed by worries over contracts and you will become increasingly expensive for grant holders to employ as your experience builds.

> There is a decades-old tradition that "the postdoc is a training ground for a tenure-track position, that this is the metric for success for young scientists," says **Cathee Phillips**, executive director of the National Postdoctoral Association (NPA). "Postdocs have heard this for years, which causes them not to think about their own strategic career plan, because they think the postdoc will naturally flow into a tenure-track position."

If you are unsure what to do, NOW would be the time to stop and think rather than use the (next) postdoc phase as a time to assess what you want. Postdoc life is hard work with rewards often linked to the amount of time and effort you put in. Coasting through the first year of a postdoc to decide if academia is for you, really doesn't help as it has not given you a true idea of what it would take to be an academic. Even non-academic employers in the future will want to know whether you have been successful during your postdoc years.

∗ Your reasons for doing a postdoc.
∗ Your reasons for not doing a postdoc.

Choosing a postdoc

So, we haven't put you off and you have made an active decision to seek a postdoc; where to start? Research is a global business and your field will have hotspots of excellence in institutions far and wide. You will need to go where the openings are; so, an understanding of who has a big grant in the pipeline, knowing which institution has just opened a new centre in your field, ensuring your network is aware that you are actively seeking a postdoc, and scanning the relevant academic job webpages are an initial set of actions. By letting people know what type of projects you are interested in, you open up the possibility of a PI employing you to work on something specific, perhaps even creating the opportunity for you to do so. If no one knows what exactly you are looking for this cannot happen.

But, given a choice of more than one, how can you make the best choice for yourself? Firstly, you may well need to apply for several (if available) postdoc positions to maximise your chances of getting a position — competition is fierce. You will probably end up applying for these in parallel. Waiting for one application to completely go through the process before looking to apply to the next is not only inefficient but you might miss some great opportunities. Academics understand this process — they have been there themselves but probably in a much less competitive market. Postdocs often worry about the "what if I get two job offers?". The answer is simple: first congratulate yourself and second decide on your options! So when applying, the best choice for you will always be tempered by the choice of positions out there in the market. However, proper research can ensure you are not wasting yours, or anyone else's, time.

It is helpful to use the 3Ps at this point: people, place and project. The 3Ps will be referred to at various points in this book and can be useful in many researcher-related decisions. The interaction between these three things can really make or break a postdoc from your point of view. Having looked at these you should have a clear idea of what this postdoc is realistically going to do for you and your career. Let's look at each of these "Ps" more closely.

People

For the most part STEM subjects are carried out in teams or research groups within departments. The people who you interact with are incredibly important. The primary person to find out about will be the PI, but think more widely about who is in the group, who works at the institute and even wider if the group is based in a large city. The best way to find out about people is to talk to some! Get several views (you don't want your decision to be made on someone else's grudge).

☐ Who am I working for? with? near?

☐ How do you know about the people you will be working with? Where have you encountered these people before?

☐ What is their world standing in your field? What is their international reputation?

☐ Will they encourage you to develop your own independent line of research and mentor you in taking the next steps in your career? Or will they expect you to act as a data-generating machine?

☐ Does the group/department work with outside collaborators (industrial or academic)?

☐ Where have previous postdocs gone on to work?

☐ How many people will I have to supervise/teach/co-ordinate?

☐ Are the above roles formally recognised?

☐ Is there training for these roles? Is there an expectation that postdocs engage with professional development opportunities?

> My reasoning is the following: Topics come and topics go; today's fashion is tomorrow's anachronism. What you do hope to find is a constant mentor who guides, helps, and supports you today and who will be there for you tomorrow and thereafter. When I was looking, I was told to dream big, but more importantly, I was told to find someone who would believe in and support my big dreams. Dreams won't always come true, but their chances of success are better if there is someone to help you make them happen. Kuan-Teh Jeang, *Yale J Biol Med*. Sep 2011; **84**(3): 191–193.

Place

Place has several levels: research group, institution and location. Location may involve more personal factors (desire to work in a given city to stay close to friends or family for instance), but the first two should be scrutinised with your full research ability. Scientific research offers opportunity for a wealth of experiences — research is a worldwide endeavour and, visas/languages permitting, the postdoc community is a very vibrant, international and mobile talent pool.

It may be tempting to stay where you are, but moving away from the institution where you studied for your PhD is really advised. You can break free of the "student" label more easily, you get further experience of another research setting, and it is easier to demonstrate research independence later on. If you are considering staying on in the same institution be very certain of your motives and be clear you are not suffering from postdoc drift. It is our experience that those who stay on in the same research group from student to postdoc rapidly become indispensable to the laboratory but their publication rate really suffers while their career ambitions become increasingly dependent on their PI.

☐ What is the institution like?
☐ What does it offer?
☐ What might it stop you doing?
☐ What equipment/libraries/resources do they have?
☐ How big is the lab? — large research groups might not provide you with all the skills you need to progress with your career, but smaller groups might lack the numbers to make an effective team. Either way you need to stay prominent in the group culture to get support and attention from your PI.
☐ Can you afford to live there? Or commute in?

Project

Finally, we get to the actual research part! Clarity on the project and what the research group has done towards it so far is incredibly important to understand. Your PhD will have been on one topic but now is the time to choose something that will add to your knowledge, put you in a good place to attract funding in a couple of years, teach you new skills and give you the best chance of publishing. If you have an idea of a future solo research project, then you could use this postdoc to build up skills or expertise to help with this future goal. Use the checklist below as a starting point.

☐ What does this project add to your CV?

☐ How does it develop your knowledge?

☐ How does it develop your skills?

☐ Is it established or untried territory?

☐ Is it aligned with the future direction of the funding bodies?

☐ Is it a new emergent area or an area that is falling out of fashion?

☐ How easy will it be to publish?

☐ Are there restrictions on publishing e.g. industrial links?

☐ Are there opportunities for collaborations/networking/conferences/reviewing/writing grants with PI as co-applicant?

☐ Are there any ethical considerations that might clash with your values?

☐ Does it excite you? (It needs to, as you will have to work hard and that excitement needs to carry you through the days when the equipment blows up.)

☐ Are there other projects in the group which can act as a back up?

☐ Will you be able to work on independent projects? (important for future career.)

☐ Who will author the papers and in which order? — find this out first!

The simple must do's before signing on the dotted line

You are about to commit a large section of your time and energy to a place so the list below should be thought about long and hard. (Hopefully, most of these will have been covered in researching the 3Ps discussed above).

- Research the group/department/institution — internet and talk to people there.
- Visit the group but also take time to investigate the place — the institution, city, campus, possible dwelling places, culture/entertainment/sport. Remember to treat any visit as if it is an interview — each and all impressions count!

- Get the low down on your potential PI from others who have worked with them
- Look at the latest Research Excellence Framework (REF) (if UK) or equivalent — how is the institution regarded? What would this mean for your CV?
- Look at the salary scale — if you were paid the bottom figure could you afford to live/commute?
- What expectations of postdocs does the institution/group have — for instance are there publishing metrics, do they have to teach?

Conclusion

These enquiries and research all take time, and good research teams will have others wanting to join them too. This means that you should be looking for the postdoc positions at least 6 months before you plan to start. A great time to start will be the "conference season" before you look to move — a chance to engage with people, demonstrate your research prowess (by presenting) and talk to others in the field.

What every postdoc needs to know about … choosing a postdoc

- ☑ It should be an active and considered decision.
- ☑ Use your research skills to consider the people, project and place.
- ☑ A postdoc is not a career but a step to the next move.

Resources

The Royal Society report "The Scientific Century: securing our prosperity," available at (https://royalsociety.org/~/media/Royal_Society_Content/policy/publications/2010/4294970126.pdf)

Ryan Wheeler, Manager, Career & Postdoctoral Services, TSRI (available at http://education.scripps.edu/postdoctoral/career_services/choosing/position.html)

Enhancing the postdoctoral experience for scientists and engineers. Available at http://www.nap.edu/read/9831/chapter/1#xii

The Research Excellence Framework (REF), available at www.ref.ac.uk

Chapter 2

The UK Higher Education Scene

Introduction

The UK has a proud history of higher education. Research has always been a strong part of this tradition. From the founding of The University of Oxford in 1096 (one of the seven "ancient" universities in the UK), then to those founded by the Royal Charter in the 1800s (e.g. The University of London), then the "red brick" universities whose original focus was science and engineering in the early 1900s (e.g. University of Leeds) through to the "plate glass" universities of the 1960s (e.g. University of Warwick) the higher education scene has evolved with the changing demands of the UK. The last great expansion was in 1992 when many polytechnic colleges became universities, e.g. Oxford Brookes University.

The majority of postdocs tend to work in higher education institutions (HEIs), while some work in public research institutes; e.g. John Innes Centre in Norwich. Additionally, some research positions equivalent to a postdoc exist in companies/business. This chapter will focus on the UK's HEIs.

Most postdocs in the UK are employed in HEIs which are funded by the government. There are over 100 institutions in the UK that are permitted to award degrees and are recognised by the UK authorities (UK and Scottish Parliament, Welsh and Northern Ireland Assemblies). The degree-awarding powers are granted by either a Royal Charter, an Act of Parliament or the Privy Council.

Not all HEIs are universities (such as some specialised art or business schools), but all UK universities are HEIs. So, what is a university? UK universities such as Oxford and Cambridge have held the title of "University" for centuries, but to gain the title of "University" now, there are a number of criteria that the institution must meet. These criteria include being granted the power to award degrees and achieving a certain number of enrolled students.

The UK has a long and evolving history of research.

Anyway, we imagine that while the history, politics and law associated with the title "university" is of interest and will help you understand some of the "interesting" viewpoints within the research community (not that academics ever have rivalries...), we need to move forward practically. So, let's get down to the realities of what you need to know.

- ☑ Which is a good university (or institution) to work for?
- ☑ Does it matter what type of university I go to? If yes, why? If no, why not?
- ☑ How do I choose?
- ☑ How will I get paid?
- ☑ What else do I need to know? i.e. I don't know what I don't know, so please help!

Which is a good university (or institution) to work for?

Well, we have our own opinions! As will anyone else you ask, so that is a good place to start: ask the opinion of your PhD supervisors, colleagues, peers and mentors. The reputation of an institution is also driven by league tables which are poured over and assessed by senior HR managers. They are dismissed if the institution has dropped down the table, and viewed positively if the institution has gone up the league table.

∗   Whose advice will you seek regarding places to work?

Universities in the UK (as is the case with all employers) vary enormously; each has differing areas of research strength, strategic aims/philosophies, working cultures, locations, size, reputation, … the list could go on and on. You will need to think about your research direction too — would you want to work somewhere that can give you a more interdisciplinary approach or are you looking to work in a particular research field. You also need to think about the next step (see later in this book) — where do alumni go on to? So, what do you want to know?

∗   What are you going to ask the people you have identified above?

Universities and research teams will change over time, meaning that the experience a colleague had of working in a certain research team 5 years ago could be vastly different to the reality today. Also career structures have changed in recent years so do take note if getting advice from older colleagues. Furthermore, as a wise old dad once said, "People love to give you their advice. Listen to it. Thank them for it. Consider it. Then do what you want!"

∗   So, while asking people is a good part of the evidence-gathering mission to find a good place to work, where else can you get some good advice and insight from?

The British Council supports "cultural relations and educational opportunities" and their webpages provide some general useful information. The Euraxess pages have a wealth of information designed to support researchers, especially those who are moving countries — also see the chapter on coming to the UK from overseas.

University league tables and the research excellence framework

There are annual league tables produced by publishers which rank universities based on criteria such as student satisfaction, employability and research quality. These include 126 UK institutions listed in the Complete University Guide and 119 UK universities listed in The Guardian's league tables. You can also look at the world rankings of universities using, for example the Times Higher Education World University Rankings.

The Research Excellence Framework (REF) and its predecessor, the Research Assessment Exercise (RAE), assess the quality of research in UK's higher education institutions. The results are used in the allocation of research funding by the government to universities. Submissions have been judged by expert review panels and judged to be either 1* (recognised nationally), 2* (recognised internationally), 3* (internationally excellent) or 4* (world-leading). The overall quality is derived from three elements — outputs, impact and environment:

Outputs: 65% of the overall results

"Outputs" are the product of any form of research. They include publications such as journal articles, monographs and chapters in books, as well as designs, performances or exhibitions.

The panels assessed the quality of outputs against the criteria of "originality, significance and rigour." The assessment was based on peer review of the outputs.

Impact: 20% of the overall results

"Impact" is any effect on, change or benefit to the economy, society, culture, public policy or services, health, the environment or quality of life, beyond academia.

Each submission included impact case studies, and an explanation of how the submitted unit had enabled impact from its research and its future strategy for impact. These were assessed in terms of the "reach and significance" of the impacts, or how far the approach and strategy are conducive to achieving impacts.

Environment: 15% of the overall results

"Environment" refers to the strategy, resources and infrastructure that support research. Submissions described the unit's research strategy; its support for research staff and students; its research income, infrastructure and facilities; and its research collaborations and wider contributions to the discipline. Universities provided data on the amount of research income they received each academic year from different types of sources, and on the number of research doctoral degrees awarded in each of these years. These were based on data that institutions report annually to the Higher Education Statistics Agency (HESA). The research environment was assessed in terms of its "vitality and sustainability."

∗ Look up the universities you are considering in the league tables and REF rankings. What position do they hold? What does this mean to you?

Please remember that while these rankings may give you some idea about how well universities perform against certain measures, they are unlikely to give you the full picture, and there is no current UK league table for the best places for postdocs to work. The Scientist has compiled a USA version and international list (which includes UK institutions) on the best places for postdocs to work. Their rankings were based on a survey of postdocs which asked questions on the following themes:

- Quality of Training and Mentoring.
- Career Development Opportunities and Networking.
- Quality of Communication.
- Value of the Postdoc Experience.
- Quality of Facilities and Infrastructure.
- Funding.
- Equity.
- Pay and Benefits.
- Family and Personal Life.

These are factors that you may want to consider when choosing an institution at which to work.

Many UK universities belong to groups or associations along with others of a similar type to promote their members' interests in research, teaching and funding. Twenty-four universities belong to The Russell Group, which is an association of research-intensive universities that formed in 1994. The University Alliance has members that are considered less research-intensive, although they will have active and excellent research facilities and opportunities that are worth exploring. Million+ is a university think-tank with a number of associates, and GuildHE represents a number of Higher Education Institutions in the UK.

In addition, there are other partnerships and groups, for example the N8 Research Partnership is a collaboration of research-intensive universities in the North of England:

- Durham University.
- Lancaster University.
- University of Leeds.
- University of Liverpool.
- University of Manchester.
- University of Newcastle.
- University of Sheffield.
- University of York.

Multinational groups include Universitas 21 which is a global network of research-intensive universities, and the League of

Russell Group	University Alliance	Million+	GuildHE
University of Birmingham	Coventry University	Abertay University	Abertay University
University of Bristol	Kingston University	Anglia Ruskin University	Arts University Bournemouth
University of Cambridge	Liverpool John Moores University	Bath Spa University	Bishop Grosseteste University
Cardiff University	Manchester Metropolitan University	Canterbury Christ Church University	Buckinghamshire New University
Durham University	Nottingham Trent University	Edinburgh Napier University	Falmouth University
University of Edinburgh	Oxford Brookes University	London Metropolitan University	Harper Adams University
University of Exeter	Plymouth University		Leeds College of Art
University of Glasgow	Sheffield Hallam University	London South Bank University	Leeds Trinity University
Imperial College London	Teesside University	Middlesex University	Newman University
King's College London	The Open University	Southampton Solent University	Norwich University of the Arts
University of Leeds	University of Brighton	Staffordshire University	Plymouth College of Art
University of Liverpool	University of Greenwich	University of Bolton	Ravensbourne
London School of Economics & Political Science	University of Hertfordshire	University of Cumbria	Rose Bruford College
University of Manchester	University of Huddersfield	University of East London	Royal Agricultural University
Newcastle University	University of Lincoln	University of Sunderland	Royal Central School of Speech and Drama

(Continued)

Table   *(Continued)*

Russell Group	University Alliance	Million+	GuildHE
University of Nottingham	University of Portsmouth	University of the Highlands and Islands	Southampton Solent University
University of Oxford	University of Salford	University of the West of Scotland	St. Mary's University College Belfast
Queen Mary University of London	University of South Wales	University of West London	St. Mary's University Twickenham
Queen's University Belfast	University of the West of England	Leeds Trinity University	Anglo European College of Chiropractic
University of Sheffield			The British School of Osteopathy
University of Southampton			The Liverpool Institute for Performing Arts
University College London			University College Birmingham
University of Warwick			University for the Creative Arts
University of York			University of Chichester
			University of St Mark & St John
			University of Suffolk
			University of Winchester
			University of Worcester
			Writtle University College
			York St. John University

European Research Universities (LERU) is a consortium of research universities in Europe. Membership in LERU is by invitation, and is evaluated against criteria such as "research volume, impact and funding, strengths in PhD training, size and disciplinary breadth, and peer-recognised academic excellence.

∗ Which groups do the universities you are considering belong to? What insights does this give you into them?

How do I choose?

There are a lot of postdocs in the UK; current estimates are around the 45,000 mark according to the HESA data. The "place" is likely to be an integral part of your decision making process in choosing your postdoc position along with "people" and "project" — see Chapter 1 "Choosing a postdoc".

∗ Which factors are important to you in choosing a place to work? Which of these are essential to you and which are "nice" but not essential?

A note on support and development

See also the Chapter 8 on skills development and opportunities.

The UK government recognised the value to the economy of research scientists in the Roberts Report "SET for success" (Roberts, 2002), but identified gaps in the skills of postgraduates and research staff, especially in applying their technical knowledge in practice, and in transferable skills. The report recommended that postdoc contract researchers should have a "clear career development plan and have access to appropriate training opportunities — for example, of at least two weeks per year." These recommendations were taken up by the Research Councils and funding was given to universities to support the training and development of researchers to fill these "gaps". This funding has since finished, but with an independent formal review and recommendation that, "Researcher development should be embedded in the normal practices of research organisations" (Hodge, 2010). The Research Councils UK was also instrumental in setting up the organisation Vitae which is, "… dedicated to realising the potential of researchers through transforming their professional and career development. We are an international programme led and managed by CRAC, a not-for-profit registered UK charity dedicated to active career learning and development."

So, there is emerging support at the UK policy level, but what about putting this support into practice through Higher Education organisations? This seems to be less robust, especially in comparison with support for doctoral research students where the Quality Assurance Agency (QAA) for Higher Education monitors standards and quality. What then are the "drivers" for postdoc support at institutional level? Policy from funders (e.g. the Wellcome Trust) and bodies such as the Royal Society in the UK are recognising the importance of supporting researchers through this postdoc transition phase by promoting more independent fellowship schemes that invest in individual researchers and not just projects. Indeed, funders are interested in knowing where the junior researchers trained within a research team are moving on to in their career. The funding agencies want to know that they are funding Principal Investigators (PIs) who are supporting the career development of their team members.

Further drivers for the promotion of supporting researcher career development come from the REF exercise where the research environment is part of the assessment. In these times of league tables and REF assessments, competition with other institutions for the best researchers continues. Imperial College, the University of Cambridge and King's College, London now have dedicated Postdoc Centres, and tailored support for postdocs and research staff helps to recruit and retain excellent researchers. Another major influence on postdoc support in institutions is the academic community itself. While many PIs are excellent managers and are supportive of training and development for their team members, the Royal Society (and others) recognises that not all PIs are. "Some responses suggest that career support courses have worked well. But there was a common feeling that attending a course 'was frowned upon by the academics'." (Royal Society, 2010).

Policy and REF assessments are all well and good, but what does this mean for you in choosing where to do your postdoc in the UK? Well, good places to work are likely to have some form of researcher/staff training, support, development, courses, workshops, events, mentoring schemes ... Investigate these through the institution's website and by asking your colleagues.

∗ What support for your career development is available?

Where does my postdoc funding come from?

You will, most likely, get paid through your institution's payroll system, but what you really need to know is where does funding for postdocs come from? Research in the UK is funded through the government, businesses (e.g. pharmaceutical companies), and private (not for profit) organisations and charities such as the Wellcome Trust (Royal Society, 2010).

> HEIs in England can apply for public funding from HEFCE, those in Wales from HEFCW, in Scotland from SFC and in Northern Ireland from DELNI. These bodies provide grant funding for the provision of education, undertaking research, and related activities. They allocate about £2 billion per year of research funding to UK universities. The REF exercise was used to assess the quality and impact of the research being conducted in UK universities, and the results are used to allocate research funding; this is termed Quality Related or QR funding.

Government funding comes to universities via government departments, the 7 Research Councils and the Higher Education

Funding Council for England (HEFCE), or its equivalent in Wales, Scotland and Northern Ireland. There are currently seven Research Councils, they are:

- Arts and Humanities Research Council (AHRC).
- Biotechnology and Biological Sciences Research Council (BBSRC).
- Engineering and Physical Sciences Research Council (EPSRC).
- Economic and Social Research Council (ESRC).
- Medical Research Council (MRC).
- Natural Environment Research Council (NERC).
- Science and Technology Facilities Council (STFC).

These seven Councils form a strategic partnership under the name of Research Councils UK (RCUK), and work with other research funders including the UK Higher Education Funding Councils, business and charities. The Research Councils get funding via the government's science budget which is allocated by the Treasury to the Department for Business, Innovation and Skills (BIS). The distribution of these funds is different to the Funding Councils (HEFCE and equivalents); the Research Councils provide funding grants for specific projects and programmes, which are awarded on the basis of applications made by individual researchers. There are a variety of different funding schemes available through the seven Research Councils and for differing career stages. As a postdoc you will be eligible to apply for some fellowship schemes, but it is likely, initially, that you will be employed as a researcher on someone else's project grant.

It is worth noting that postdoc pay may vary slightly from place to place (London Universities will often have a London weighting to compensate for a higher cost of living in the capital). Many postdocs will often overlook the other employment benefits when looking at a new post. Holiday entitlement, childcare schemes, transportation loans, etc. will vary significantly from institution to institution and can be of considerable financial value.

Fixed term and open-ended contracts

A postdoc is not a job for life. Research is funded by grants which are for a set length of time; therefore, the employment of people on these grants will be dictated by this time frame. Hence, the majority of postdocs are on a fixed-term employment contract. These contracts can vary in length from, the very unhelpful, 6 months (usually these are using up funds after a previous postdoc has left) to 5 years on some large programme grants.

Those working on a fixed-term contract should be treated comparably with those on "permanent" or open-ended contracts, which means that contract research staff should not be adversely affected in terms of e.g. access to services or employee benefits because of their contract status. It should be noted that we, the authors, prefer the term open-ended contract because a permanent employee can always be made redundant. In 2002, the Fixed Term Employee regulations became part of UK law following an EC directive on Fixed Term Work. The University and College Union (UCU) explain a key point that affects postdocs:

"The regulations limit the use of successive fixed-term contracts to a period of 4 years. Once a fixed-term employee has 4 years' continuous service on two or more contracts (or has had their contract renewed), the contract automatically becomes indefinite unless the continued use is objectively justified." (UCU commentary on the Fixed Term Employees (Prevention of Less Favourable Treatment) Regulations 2002).

Again, we regret to point out that "indefinite" does not mean forever or permanent. If the grant that employs you comes to an end then, chances are, you will be made redundant. Where this legislation does help postdocs is that they should now be entitled to redundancy payments and any redeployment services that their institution offers. All the information you need on this will be available through your institution's Human Resources (HR) service. Although the contract end may seem a long way off it is wise to understand what may happen when the contract stops (and hopefully this will spur you on to finding the next position!)

What else do I need to know?

- The UK Higher Education system is not a static being; it is constantly evolving and changing. The undergraduate system has changed dramatically in the last 20 years with the introduction of tuition fees and increasing numbers of students going to university.
- There is an increased appetite for the public to be kept informed of the research that they are funding through their taxes via the government, and, in many cases, to be involved in the design and development of the research.
- Funding from all sources for research is limited and competitive.
- UK HEIs include some of the best places in the world to do research (according to various league tables ... and also according to the highly biased authors!)

Conclusion

The UK Higher Education scene has a long history and solid research foundations. With changes in UK research funding and the wider world, universities and other research institutions are constantly evolving and, if you are reading this book several years after its publication, things like REF and HEFCE may well have mutated into new "beasts"! (Changes are afoot as we publish). Some understanding or appreciation of the political and economic situation within which academic and postdoc research is conducted in the UK may help you to understand more practical day-to-day aspects of your job, such as how you get paid and why you are likely employed on a fixed-term contract. Therefore, some background research on these aspects is highly advised.

What every postdoc needs to know about ... the UK Higher Education scene

- ☑ Research continues to be a strong part within the UK's long tradition of higher education, which is a sector that is constantly evolving and changing.

☑ Support and development opportunities for postdocs within the UK HEIs are varied and form part of the institutions' strategies to attract and retain great researchers (who will carry out great research that is associated with their institution). Find out what is on offer at places you plan to apply to.

☑ All employers differ, HEIs in the UK are included in this. Oxford is very different to Cambridge (which they are at constant lengths to prove, not least by the annual boat race on The River Thames), and these institutions differ dramatically to Imperial, Surrey, and Liverpool. The point being that your postdoc experience will be shaped by the place you choose to do it, so it is worth investigating the options.

Resources

HODGE, A. 2010. Review of progress in implementing the recommendations of Sir Gareth Roberts, regarding employability and career development of PhD students and research staff. A report for Research Councils UK by an Independent Review Panel.

ROBERTS, G. 2002. SET for success. The supply of people with science, technology, engineering and mathematics skills.

ROYAL SOCIETY 2010. The Scientific Century: securing our future prosperity. The Royal Society.

Research Councils UK, available at (http://www.rcuk.ac.uk/)

HEFCE, available at http://www.hefce.ac.uk/

The British Council, available at http://www.britishcouncil.org/

Euraxess, available at, http://www.britishcouncil.org/study-work-create/opportunity/research-collaboration/euraxess

Complete University Guide, available at http://www.thecompleteuniversityguide.co.uk/

The Guardian league table, available at http://www.theguardian.com/education/universityguide

Times Higher Education World rankings, available at https://www.timeshighereducation.co.uk/world-university-rankings

The Research Excellence Framework (REF), available at http://www.ref.ac.uk/

The Scientist, available at http://www.the-scientist.com/

The Russell group, available at http://www.russellgroup.ac.uk

The University Alliance, available at http://www.unialliance.ac.uk/ about/

Million+, available at http://www.millionplus.ac.uk

GuildHE, available at http://www.guildhe.ac.uk

League of European Research Universities (LERU), available at http:// www.leru.org/index.php/public/home/

Vitae, available at https://www.vitae.ac.uk/

The University and College Union (UCU) on fixed term regulations, available at http://www.ucu.org.uk/ftregs

Chapter 3

Coming to the UK as a Researcher — With Lessons for Those Going Overseas

Introduction

With its wealth of high quality research-intensive universities and its history of groundbreaking scientific innovation, the UK attracts many overseas researchers. UK universities are increasingly places with a vibrant international mix bringing a diversity in educational methods, cultures and working patterns to research. This can foster a creative, lively place in which to explore and challenge the boundaries of science and technology. The variety of universities from ancient to modern stems from a tradition of valuing education. Our chapter on the UK higher education (HE) scene covers this in more detail.

If you are looking for research jobs in the UK then the jobs.ac.uk website is used by most universities to advertise posts. It also offers careers advice webpages, videos and country profiles covering the cost of living, working practices and professional etiquette.

The UK also has much to offer as a place to live and explore with historical, cultural and natural wonders within our relatively small islands and ready access to continental Europe. This chapter will help you navigate moving to the UK but its lessons could easily be taken on board by postdocs moving to other countries.

* What worries you most about coming to the UK (or going to a different country)? How could you address this?

Considering the UK

What do you need to think about if you find a great postdoc position in the UK? If you are considering a move to the UK, there are some standard questions to ask yourself, which would also apply to UK nationals thinking of postdocs elsewhere in the world. Use the checklist below to explore some of the key topics. If you are unsure of anything this should be your prompt to investigate further.

☐ Do you need a visa/permit to work in the UK?
The best place to start is the UK Government website.

☐ Will the research institution help you with this?
Most universities are familiar with the visa process (although individual Principal Investigators (PIs) may not be). Ask to be put in contact with someone from Human Resources (HR). The Science without Borders site has some guidance.

☐ Do you understand the cost of living at the research institution you are looking at?
You need to investigate your likely salary, taxes, where people live, whether/how they commute, childcare costs. The cost of living can vary greatly throughout the UK and across London. London weighting[1] (see Resources for the definition of London weighting) is often added to salaries in central London universities. A good guide can be found at the Work Gateways site but asking other postdocs at your proposed institution will yield the best information.

☐ Where will I live? Can your employer provide interim accommodation whilst you settle?
Some universities can provide temporary accommodation (possibly student rooms that are available over the summer

---

[1] **London weighting** (from Wikipedia) is an allowance paid to certain civil servants, teachers, airline employees, PhD students, police and security officers in and around London, the capital of the United Kingdom. It is designed to help these workers with the cost of living in Greater London, which is higher than that of the rest of the UK. Its purpose is to encourage key workers to stay in Greater London.

holiday for instance). Do not assume this is the case though. Find out about renting a place to live through your institute's accommodation office (or similar — this may be under student services, staff services or an overseas support unit — hunt through the institution's website or ask HR). You may want to consider Airbnb as a temporary option for when you first arrive; this would then give you time to explore the area and view rooms or properties to rent.

☐ Are there systems to support newcomers to the institution/city? Most universities will have some formal induction event but this may only run termly or even annually. Your PI should provide you with all the essential information (health & safety, laboratory procedures, work plan, research group induction). Seek out any postdoc societies (if there are any), Student's Union or HR to ask about wider induction and familiarisation. Check if there is a mentoring or buddy scheme in place to support new members of staff. In some instances, universities may be able to help with relocation costs; while this is usually reserved for more senior members of staff it might be worth asking! Universities usually have an International Office or something similar that will provide information for students arriving from overseas; while all of this information may not be relevant to you as a member of staff, there is likely to be some useful information and it is a good place to start.

☐ Do you know anyone nearby?
Changing job and country at the same time can be a huge challenge. Identifying people you know (or can connect with through your network) to provide a friendly face could be very helpful.

☐ Are there others from your country/culture at the institute? Many universities have student/staff led societies promoting and supporting those who have travelled to the UK. These offer good networking opportunities, support and advice, as well as social events.

☐ Is there support for those you might be bringing with you?
If you are planning to bring your family with you, then you must consider the visa formalities. Additionally, you may need

to consider other factors such as friends and support for your partner, nurseries or schools for your children. A good example of support given by a university is Cambridge's Newcomers and Visiting Scholars — there may well be something similar at the institution you are considering. There may well be an association of researchers from your country in the UK (for instance The Society of Spanish Researchers in the UK).

☐ Are my English language skills good enough?
"International postdocs listed language as a MAJOR barrier encountered when transitioning to the US." (Johns Hopkins Postdoctoral Association). Whilst most universities offer support for both spoken and written English, a good standard of English will be expected and will make your transition much easier. Consider taking steps to strengthen your English before you come to the UK — it will benefit your research and everyday life.

Ivana's story

I decided to move from Austria to the UK in 2012 as a postdoc when my boyfriend relocated. I have found research in the UK to be very international and a great place to exchange ideas and make contacts. Most people don't care where you are from just what you can do. UK universities are also well known and highly regarded. I strongly believe a postdoc in a good group at a good university will always be beneficial to your prospects. The main challenges I have found were bureaucracy: I needed to know a lot more about Visas and ensure the university could fill everything out correctly. I also had to take an English test despite having studied partly in English. I wish I had known that people do not necessarily expect you to have publications to apply for a postdoc in the UK. My advice would be to be patient and determined. There is a lot of hassle with paperwork. Also, if you are coming from a small, unknown place people can be snobbish and ask you many silly questions. Don't take things too personally.

Action plan for settling in

Integration with those around you will help you settle into your new role and also get the most from working in the UK. At first you may want to "throw yourself into the work," but getting to know who you are working with and what resources the location has to offer as soon as possible will pay dividends as you progress. You may not be naturally outgoing but making the first step can be important. Some suggestions for activities are below:

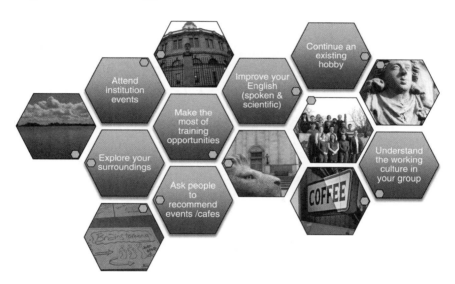

Remember that English is the primary language spoken in UK universities. It is expected that day-to-day business will be conducted in English. If you have colleagues who share a language, social interactions in that language may be appropriate but it is polite to ensure that no individual or group are excluded. Everyone, and the research, suffers if people form cliques within a group defined by culture or language.

Practicalities and paperwork

Banking can be a challenge to set up in the UK for someone who has just arrived and doesn't have a permanent address. Our best advice is to seek help from your PI and local postdocs before you arrive so you are prepared to find a bank account and can therefore rent somewhere to live.

Upon arrival, you should register with a **National Health Service (NHS) doctor** as soon as possible (don't wait until you fall ill); your institution may have a medical centre that you can register with or they should be able to provide lists of doctors' surgeries. You can also check the NHS webpages. **Dentists** in the UK rarely take on NHS (reduced cost) patients and so you may want to consider health insurance. Registering with a dentist is separate from registering with a doctor.

It would be wise to familiarise yourself with **driving and/or cycling** rules in the UK. It also helps when walking around our large cities. These are covered in The Highway Code. Rail information can be found online at National Rail Enquiries and general public transport links can be found on Traveline (see Resources at the end of this chapter).

Emergency services in the UK include the police, ambulance and fire services as well as the coastguard. To contact them in an emergency you should dial 999. In England in a non-emergency situation, or if you are unsure whether you need to go to hospital, you can dial 111.

Television (TV) licence — you must have a valid TV licence to watch or record television. This also applies if you are a tenant or lodger, and includes the use of a computer, mobile phone, games console, digital box or DVD/VHS recorder to watch programmes.

Council tax is payable on the property where you live and covers council services. In the UK the Council Tax is the responsibility of the tenant (that is you!) not the landlord.

Utilities — gas, electricity and water. If you are renting a room or property check whether the energy and utility bills are included in the rental costs. If not, you will need to contact the companies and arrange payment. Further advice can be found on energy company websites or via the Citizen's Advice service pages (see Resources).

British peculiarities!

British culture and habits may be very different to those you are used to. Shaking hands is the norm for meeting people for the first time, especially in a formal setting. Britain is also steeped in history and its calendar events reflect this. The following books may help understand both the British and their culture: "Watching the English: The Hidden Rules of English Behaviour" by Kate Fox, and "Britty Britty Bang Bang: One Man's Attempt to Understand His Country" by Hugh Dennis. These will cover the topics of queuing, talking about the weather, pantomimes, Bonfire night, and the over-use of the word "sorry", which are all peculiarities of the British.

> "I wish I had known more about British culture; at first I assumed that Germans and Brits are similar. I experienced the cultural similarity paradox — members of the British culture are some-times vague and very complicated to work with (from a German point of view). I should have learned about my own cultural fingerprint to be able to better understand the British culture."

The British will always talk about the weather but don't blame us, blame the Gulf Stream!

Things to spend your annual leave on

Getting postdocs to take all their holiday entitlement (annual leave) always seems a struggle! The UK has a lot to offer outside the research environment — a rich history and a wide range of cultures. As a member of staff you will have an annual leave entitlement (variable from place to place but UK Universities typically offer postdocs over 30 days leave a year) which may be in addition to National (Bank) Holidays which are primarily around Christian festivals. Your research requires an inquisitive mindset and with lots to explore in the UK we would encourage you to take your full leave entitlement! Here are some ideas:

- Museums and galleries.
- Concerts, plays, musicals, cinemas.
- Football, cricket, rugby, golf and other sporting events.
- Leisure centres — including swimming, ice-skating, ten-pin bowling.
- Festivals and other music events.
- Special days — Bonfire Night on the 5th November is uniquely British.
- City parks and gardens.
- National parks and stunning landscapes including the Peak District, Snowdonia, the Lake District, the Yorkshire Moors, Dartmoor, the Norfolk Broads, the Scottish Highlands, the Cornish coastline, the Cotswolds and the New Forest.
- Historic buildings and monuments (look at The National Trust/English Heritage sites).
- Pubs, clubs and restaurants.
- Students' union — clubs, events, societies (most will include postdocs).
- Postdoc events.

Help from the European Union

The European Union (EU) offers help to researchers who want to pursue research within the boundaries of the EU to both EU nationals and those from outside the Union via the Euraxess website. This is a source for information on social security, health care, work permits, schooling (if you are bringing your family) and much more. This is a great place to start investigating. Each member of this network has a contact at the university that you can email and will help with your queries about moving. They will help to put you in touch with the right teams at the university to assist you with specific queries. It should be noted that different EU states have different systems for taxation, social security, etc.

The United Kingdom's status in/with the EU is evolving following the 2016 referendum so we would recommend looking closely at partnerships/schemes/directives. See the resources section for links.

Conclusion

Moving job can be a huge change and if you couple that with changing country you are bound to feel somewhat stressed at times. However, there is help and support for those coming to the UK and the UK has much to offer the postdoc researcher. We all work in institutions with a great cultural mix and would encourage you to seriously consider making the UK your destination!

What every postdoc needs to know about …
coming to the UK

- ☑ Use your research skills to find out as much as you can about the UK.
- ☑ Embrace opportunities to explore new places and meet new people.
- ☑ Do not blame us for the weather!

Resources

UK Academic job site http://www.jobs.ac.uk/careers-advice/country-profiles/united-kingdom.

UK Government website, available at https://www.gov.uk/check-uk-visa.

Family Visas, available at https://www.gov.uk/tier-5-government-authorised-exchange/family-members.

The Work Gateways, available at http://www.workgateways.com/working-in-the-uk/cost-of-living.

Air B&B, available at https://www.airbnb.co.uk.

Cambridge's Newcomers and Visiting Scholars, available at http://www.nvs.admin.cam.ac.uk.

The Society of Spanish Researchers in the UK, available at http://www.sruk.org.uk.

National Health Service (NHS) www.nhs.uk

The Highway Code, available at https://www.gov.uk/browse/driving/highway-code.

National Rail Enquiries, available at http://www.nationalrail.co.uk.

General public transport Travelline, available at http://www.traveline.info.

Television license, available at http://www.tvlicensing.co.uk/.

Council tax information, available at https://www.gov.uk/council-tax.

British holidays, available at https://www.gov.uk/bank-holidays.

Euraxess supports a scientific visa scheme, available at http://ec.europa.eu/euraxess/index.cfm/services/scientificVisa.

Euraxess pension scheme — single European pension arrangement.

UK Citizen's Advice, available at https://www.citizensadvice.org.uk/

"Watching the English: The Hidden Rules of English Behaviour" by Kate Fox.

"Britty Britty Bang Bang: One Man's Attempt to Understand His Country" by Hugh Dennis.

Chapter 4

How to get the Most out of Your Postdoc

Why are you doing a postdoc?

The first step in getting the most out of your postdoc is to know why you are doing it. You may have succumbed to "postdoc drift" and stumbled into the role by default; someone down the corridor had a position coming up, asked you if you would like to do it, and a few weeks later you are employed as a postdoc researcher without having consciously decided that's what you wanted to do. Alternately, you may have painstakingly researched and targeted a particular institution and research team, tracked opportunities and applied for a position; then meticulously prepared for the interview before landing your dream job. Most people will be somewhere between these two. Whichever way you ended up in your postdoc job, it is then important to consider *why* you are doing it.

∗ So, why *are* you doing your postdoc? To (Please tick all that apply):

☐ Enhance my publication/research record.
☐ Build collaborations and networks.
☐ Develop my technical or research expertise.
☐ Pay the mortgage/rent.

☐ Try out teaching in an academic environment.
☐ Develop the skills I think I need to get a "permanent" academic position.
☐ Build my personal profile within the research community.
☐ Enhance my CV.
☐ Feed my desire to do fabulous research in an area/discipline I love.
☐ Continue working in a university/higher education establishment.
☐ Continue working in the same location.
☐ Develop knowledge or skills that I can transfer to industry or to the commercial sector.
☐ Work in a different country/place.
☐ Learn a new language.
☐ Build my independence as a researcher.
☐ Help me work out what I want to do next.
☐ Other — what did we miss? …

What does a successful postdoc look like?

The answer to this will depend on who you ask and what you define as "successful"! Here are some viewpoints:

Your Principal Investigator (PI) is likely to view a successful postdoc as one who publishes, produces data/results/research outputs that link with the funded project. They may also view success in terms of helping/mentoring other researchers within the team and contributing to the overall team "performance".

Your funding body[1] is likely to view a successful postdoc as one who produces outputs (conference presentations, research papers, media stories) with the name of the funding body attached, i.e. Dr Science funded by XXXX has discovered YYYY.

---

[1] Unsure who this is? Find out! It isn't just your institution. The research money will come from a research council, charity or something similar.

Your peers and colleagues — how do you know if your colleagues are successful? We tend to judge our progress against others based on the external measures imposed by our PIs and the academic environment, i.e. research papers and outputs. We may also judge them based on what job they move onto next. They may well judge you too! But by opening up a conversation along these lines, you could find, reassuringly, you are all in the same boat.

You — this is the most important question to answer, "What does a successful postdoc position mean to me?" You are likely to rely on the parameters put in place by the people and organisations listed above, i.e. getting data, results, publications … These things fit nicely with the needs of your PI, but when it comes to raising your profile, networking, attending seminars, going to conferences, training in research leadership and management, or finding your next job then there can be a clash with the expectations of your PI. This potential conflict of interests is further explored in the section on the relationship between you and your PI.

Our thoughts — In our experience, successful postdocs are pro-active and organised. They seek opportunities to expand their experience and skills. They are realistic. They know when their contract will end and do not rely on vague promises of further funding, but go out and get their own funding or find another job. Successful postdocs are excellent at managing their time and are able to devote energy to the "important but not urgent" work including attending seminars and nurturing collaborations, whilst resisting the "time bandits" such as answering emails or rearranging the lab. We view success as a postdoc being able to take the next career step confidently, with the skills they need and a network to support them — whatever future career they choose.

∗ How will *you* know if *your* time as a postdoc has been success-ful? Note down your measures of success.

Ingredients of a successful postdoc

As with all recipes, the balance of ingredients is key but will be personal to your tastes and career direction. The following are the ingredients that we encounter in successful postdocs. Many of these can be refined by attending training courses, learning from those around you and building on your experience. All highlight that being a successful postdoc is not an easy option!

The balance of ingredients will be key to making your postdoc successful for you.

Doing excellent research and becoming an independent researcher

A postdoc position is often considered to be a step on the road to becoming a fully independent researcher. Excellent research doesn't land in peoples' lap and has much more to do with perseverance than luck. Therefore, you will need to have a publication plan, a project plan, and a personal career development plan. Lots of plans! Many researchers are resistant to the idea of planning because they know they will change and so don't see the value in planning to start with. This circular argument can be counteracted by another circular argument: the first rule of planning is to have a plan. The second rule is that it will change. But if you don't have a plan, you can't change it. Convinced? Thought not. In our experience, those postdocs who have planning skills fare better than those who don't.

Publication plans

You will need a strategy for publishing your work. Advertising your work to the academic community as well as any other stakeholders such as patient groups, charities funding your work, UK taxpayers, and industry partners is hugely important in establishing yourself as a successful researcher. The skills and experience of doing this is valuable for a multitude of future career options. In the academic world, peer-reviewed publications are a major criterion by which researchers are assessed. Please see Chapter 6 for further information.

Project plans and time management

A research project needs careful project management to be successful, and this is a role that you will naturally take on for your own work and maybe for others in the research team in which you work. You will likely be employed on a fixed-term contract so, you will need to work within a set time frame and be realistic about what can be achieved in that time. It may be that follow-on funding becomes available or is promised for your research, but you should not rely on this.

The first place to start is the grant from which you are funded. Ensure you have a copy! Reading this will give you a good overview and should outline clear deliverables and the impact of the project. If you are joining a project part way through, ask to read the grant and gain an understanding of what stage the project has reached from your PI. Then, when planning your part of the project consider:

☑ What reading do you need to do to get up to speed?
☑ Do you need any technical training?

☑ Is all the equipment in place/operational?
☑ Are all the consumables available?
☑ Is your role dependent on someone else doing work?
☑ What time do you need to allow for contingencies?

Having a clear project plan is not only important for you to get the most out of your research time on a postdoc contract, it also has implications for research integrity and data management issues. Carrying out research following agreed and careful plans helps to avoid sloppy research which in turn could produce misleading data and outputs that get published. You only need to briefly look at the Retraction Watch website to scare yourself into getting your project plan organised!

Time management is one of our favourite postdoc courses to run because several people always turn up late! (Indeed one person turned up half an hour after the workshop had finished!) But seriously, it is a subject that many postdocs struggle with. Postdocs "suffer" from two things: many calls on their time, and typically unstructured days/nights in which to work. However, the solution to this is to embrace the reality and view postdoc life as being blessed with a varied, interesting, demanding job and a large amount of freedom to organise one's work. This is often not true of other roles. But the freedom does need structuring.

Ask yourself, when do you work best? This is the time of day that you should dedicate to the really important career enhancing things you need to do. This "golden time" should be used to write papers, apply for grants, think creatively, do that tough piece of analysis… Ideally, this time should be block booked for you.

∗ When is golden time for you?

You also may need to consider *how* you organise your time (not what you do). Our advice would be to use one diary for everything and preferably make that diary electronic. Why one diary? Because increasingly work and life outside come very close and avoiding clashes ensures you let no-one down. Why electronic? Chances are you are nearly always near your mobile or a computer of some sort and electronic diaries make it very easy to do the following time (or face) saving activities:

☑ Have multiple calendars (for different projects, family members, etc.).
☑ Allow for searching.
☑ Allow you to subscribe to calendars (for seminars, institution events, etc.).
☑ Link to emails making it possible to have all the details of a meeting linked to the event.
☑ Allow easy sharing with others (colleagues, family, etc.).
☑ Set reminders for events.
☑ Link to planning tools.
☑ A visual check on what is taking up your time.

Obviously, a calendar is only useful if you use it. It can contain bookings for yourself (such as a block of writing time) as well as appointments with others. It can also be used to track how you are spending your time if you are wondering where the working day disappears to (there are apps/programs that can do this too). Sharing your calendar may well bring benefits such as people not disturbing you when you are writing (or even encouraging you to write because your diary has advertised to everyone the fact that you should be writing!).

So, how to fill the diary when it is up to you? We have found the Pomodoro Technique[2] very helpful. This is a method of dividing up work using blocks of time measured using a traditional tomato ticking kitchen timer (although any timer works and you can use online versions). The standard block is 25 mins long followed by a short break. The focus for those 25 mins should be the task in hand and nothing else. Cirillo (the author of this technique) combines this working method efficiently with a daily action list in his book, but we find the focus is the really useful part. So, when it comes to booking appointments with yourself in your diary we would recommend blocks of time for which you can really focus. A good tip

---

[2] The Pomodoro Technique Francesco Cirillo.

is also to start getting a measure of how long it takes to do things — this way your "review a paper slot" will be an accurate timing rather than an optimistic half hour. A few days spent listing what you do and when will give you a better idea of where your time goes and any particular "bandits" that steal your time.

Using to-do lists, action lists, planners can help keep track of "jobs" that need to be done but can often miss out on the big stuff. How often do we write on a to-do list "consider career" or "blue sky thinking for next research direction?" And yet if we don't do these things we can't make our postdoc successful because we don't know where we are aiming. A simple way to combat this is to ensure we do what is important (to us) as well as what is urgent (usually PI demands!). The grid below illustrates this:

	Urgent	This week	This month
Very important	If everything is in this box — panic!	←	←
Moderately important	↑	↖	↖
Needs considering	↑	↖	Ensure these get moved across/up

Many to-do list apps now incorporate an importance rating and the deadline, so they can be used to tell you what to do and when!

One particular bandit that steals big chunks of our time is email. For a tool that is supposed to help us, we think sometimes it is driving our behaviour. There are many techniques for dealing with emails but we have found the following most useful in day to day institutional life:

☑ Practice the 3Ds with any incoming email.
   ○ **Do it** — quick tasks that take 5 mins or less.
   ○ **Diarise it** — drag and drop this email into your diary and set a time to do it (tasks like reviewing a paper or reading a document).
   ○ **Delete it** — if not relevant.

☑ Unsubscribe to anything not helpful and/or you don't read (email groups, LinkedIn lists, shopping emails…).

☑ Use your email system's folders/rules to good effect making things easy to find.

☑ Check your email at specific times rather than constantly.

☑ Limit your time on email.

☑ Ensure you have a professional signature which gives your contact details.

☑ Clear out your inbox occasionally.

☑ Do not check your email late at night/early morning.

☑ Always think — would this be quicker picking up the phone?

Another concern for postdocs is Masters and PhD students taking up much of their time. Keeping "office hours" might be hard to do in an open plan research space, but trying to encourage students to come to you at specific times is helpful for you and also for them as it encourages a bit more independent thought rather than being given an answer straight away. Also ensure this time is not your golden time and is a time that suits you. Encourage people to respect your time by publicising your plans ("I write from 9 to 10 each morning") and reminding them of this (I'm writing now, can you find me after 10-am please?). People will soon get used to your schedule (and may even copy you when the papers start churning out!).

If a PI comes to you frequently with demands on your time then it is much harder to say "no". However, if you are in control of your schedule it will be very easy to communicate the implications of taking on a last minute task. "I can take on that paper review but this will delay the abstract for the conference we had hoped to present at." Being a postdoc is hard work and sometimes demands long hours but there are only so many days in the week and hours in the day. Some of the best time management lessons can be learnt from those who work part time for whatever reason. Often these people pack more into their hours at work because they cannot stay later or take work home. The old saying "If you want something doing ask a busy person" is well worth remembering here.

Thinking ahead: Personal and career development plan

"Being a postdoc is not a career" is a commonly used phrase that postdocs should embrace. Therefore, one measure of success that often gets overlooked is finding the next job. You should therefore be looking to enhance, develop and gain the skills and experience required for the next step in your career, be that in academia or in the thousands of other fabulous options that are available to the highly skilled pool of researchers to which you belong. You therefore need to consider the skills that employers are looking for, know which skills you possess and which you need to develop, and have a plan for tackling this. Please see the later sections of the book for CV advice but note that this stage should be considered *during* your postdoc to give you time to enhance your CV appropriately.

Raising your profile

Whether you end up staying in academia or moving to one of the thousands of other career options, the network of contacts you build up can be invaluable. Getting the most out of your postdoc involves raising your profile, and both getting to know people and being known by others. See section on "Raising your profile and creating opportunities" in Chapter 8.

Some suggestions on how to raise your profile:

- ☑ Publish!
- ☑ Increase your citations.
- ☑ Widening participation or public engagement activities.
- ☑ Present your work at conferences — locally, nationally, internationally.
- ☑ Update your university webpages.
- ☑ Consider social media outlets for advertising your work.
- ☑ Add a signature at the bottom on your emails that includes a link to your latest journal article/book/conference presentation.
- ☑ Attend seminars and ask questions.

☑ Volunteer for committees.
☑ Get involved with teaching.
☑ Organise events for postdocs e.g. arrange for someone to come and talk in your department about CVs, preparing funding bids, or arrange a networking coffee session.
☑ Set up a journal club or reading group.
☑ Attend staff development events.

Trying things out

Getting the most out of your postdoc also means testing options and trying things out. These could include public engagement activities, teaching, managing student projects or enrolling on research management training, preparing funding bids or being involved in your PI's bids to gain an understanding of the process, sitting on university or departmental committees, setting up seminar series, or running a journal club/reading group for doctoral students. Many institutions now offer the chance to become informed and/or involved in entrepreneurial ventures. As a postdoc you can tap into what your institution offers for staff in terms of professional development and sometimes access those events designed for research students. Our advice would be to make the most of what is on offer to you, it will certainly cost you much more to access training through online or evening courses once you have left the institution.

Limits and practicalities

Most postdocs are working on fixed-term contracts meaning that there is an end date to your contract of employment. After considering why you are doing your postdoc, you need to consider the time frame that you are working in. Also, you will most likely have been employed to do a certain piece of research work within a research project that has milestones and deliverables. Both time and the research project may be limits on the things you identified above. For example, if you wanted to try out teaching, this may be limited if you are only on a 6 month contract although we would encourage you to undertake at least some teaching. Also once you have experience of, for example, committee work evidenced on your CV you do not need to become a life-long member of the committee — do your best and then hand on the reigns to someone new.

✳ Think about what career you would like to follow and the skills you want to enhance

Conclusion

Being a postdoc is not a career (sorry to repeat this again), so you must focus on getting the most out of your (usually) fixed amount of time at your institution. If doing a postdoc is likened to baking: to make a cake you need to know what cake you are aiming to make, and for a postdoc you need to know what a successful post-doc means for you. For the cake you need to have the recipe, for a postdoc you need to have a project and career plan. For the cake, ingredients need to be combined and cooked in the right way, for a postdoc you need to combine the opportunities provided in your environment that fit with your plan. For the cake, you need to cook it for the right amount of time, and for a postdoc all this needs to fit in the time of your fixed-term contract. For the cake, don't burn it; for the postdoc, have an exit plan!

What every postdoc needs to know about ... getting the most out of your time as postdoc

☑ Know why you are doing a postdoc and what you would like to get out of the time.

☑ Take advantage of any opportunities for training, development, sitting on committees, entrepreneurial schemes, teaching, mentoring ...

☑ Try things out and explore options to help you succeed in your career plans.

Resources

The Pomodoro Technique, available at http://pomodorotechnique.com.

UK Research Integrity Office UKRIO, available at http://ukrio.org.

Retraction Watch, available at http://retractionwatch.com.

Raising your academic profile, available at http://www.jobs.ac.uk/careers-advice/working-in-higher-education/1933/how-to-raise-your-international-academic-profile

Chapter 5

The Relationship with your Principal Investigator

Introduction

In order to build a good and productive working environment it is important that the line manager/employee relationship is the most effective it can be. In the case of postdocs, your line manager is usually also the Principal Investigator (PI) on the project you have been employed to work on. The research project grant they have employed you to work on is likely to have been gained competitively through the hard work, commitment and expertise of the PI.

A good relationship with your PI will be invaluable, now and in the future. Not only will they be a referee for you, they could also be a life-long colleague, mentor and collaborator. Whatever the career direction you are heading in, this person will be part of your network and in turn you can access their network. It is therefore important to ensure that this relationship works. This chapter aims to help you with this.

...It's complicated!

We believe that the postdoc/PI relationship is the most complex in higher education (HE). Both parties are heavily reliant upon each other: the success of the PI's career is dependent upon successful research and the completion of the research project. The postdoc also needs the project to be successful so they can move onto the next step in their career. The problem lies in the definition of success for both parties.

Elements of success that they will both share will be:

- Publications (quality and quantity).
- Profile raising (presenting at conferences, talks to other groups).

The PI will also be looking for:

- Improved standing in the Research Excellence Framework (REF).
- Students successfully supervised to the end of masters/PhD programmes.
- Ability to apply for further grants.
- Collaboration opportunities.

The postdoc will also be looking for (regardless of career direction):

- Technique/research skills development.
- Networking opportunities.
- CV building.
- Securing the next position.

However, it is not a relationship of equals; the postdoc has a fixed-term contract and needs to plan for their next career move, and a good PI will be a good line manager and encourage the postdoc to think of their next career move. Yet, it is not in the PI's interest for a good postdoc to leave before the end of the contract. But … a good postdoc will also be thinking of their career and will need to put themselves first and may have to start planning their next move within the final year of the project.

So … it's complicated! However, building a good relationship comes down to one key factor: clear and open communication.

* Think about your PI's career: was your PI a postdoc? How long ago? How did they get to be here?

What PIs really think

Knowing how complex this relationship is and how challenging it can be, we asked a number of PIs at Imperial College London a series of questions about their working relationships with their postdocs. The PIs replied in general terms (there was no naming and shaming) and their thoughts will be explored here with the mission of what, as a postdoc, you can do to build a productive working relationship. Whilst reading think about your own behaviours and interactions. If you spot any contradictions, keep in mind that PIs are all unique human beings (yes, most are human!) with a spectrum of beliefs and attitudes.

How does your ideal postdoc behave?

"Self-motivated, dynamic, enthusiastic, ability to drive the project forward, reads the literature, communicates well with me and the group. Technically competent. Good team player, but at the same time focused and prioritises their own work. Helpful to others in the lab (but does not become the lab technician). Efficient, hard working, will go the extra mile. Thinks about their project and is genuinely interested in their project."

"The ideal postdoc is able to run with ideas, and so following a weekly meeting with their [PI] will then take those ideas that are agreed and discussed and develop them independently. They can be pointed in the direction of someone that can help, and then be trusted to make the contact. The postdoc will be able to operate independently however they will not go 'AWOL' and will contact the [PI] if there is a problem or something needs discussing."

"Keen, enthusiastic, listening to advice, hard working, proactive without overstepping the mark, eager to help outside the remit of their own particular project."

What makes an ideal postdoc?

"Someone who sees that they are developing into an independent scientist and wants to be independent, but recognises that the [PI] has something to contribute!"

"A degree of energy and hard work. This does not mean long hours outside normal working time (though sometimes it might). It means that they work hard and in an organised and focused way when they are in work. I do not want someone that works 10.30 am–8 pm (not an unusual working pattern!) but spends 40% of their time on Facebook! I would prefer someone that worked 9–5 but packed their day and always asked 'what experiments can I do in this time'."

"Enthusiasm and willingness to take on challenges. Self starting"

What behaviours do you find most frustrating?

"Postdocs who show no initiative, are unmotivated, need spoon feeding, spend all day on Facebook and other non-work related sites, 9–5 working mentality. Social life takes priority over work life. The lazy postdoc who doesn't care about their experiments. The arrogant postdoc who does not appreciate your wealth of knowledge and expertise."

"Someone that just brings negative problems/moans all the time and expects you to solve them."

"Someone who is always demanding 'goodies' (to go on conferences, to have some expensive kits to do research) but is not willing to do any of the background work to either. (i) justify going on the conference (i.e. getting data) or (ii) about what they want to do (i.e. they can ask for kit to do the research but not know the price, how the kit works, what the alternatives are). I think what I am saying is a postdoc who expects the supervisor to be a combination of a loving mother who will cure all ills and a wizard with a magic wand."

"Someone who does not engage in the science."

"Bad timekeeping, lack of written protocols and ineffective feedback on experiments, lazy, not pro-active and thinking ahead to the next step, not able to listen and take advice."

The postdocs you have had a good relationship with — what are the key characteristics of that relationship?

"Good communication (i.e. they keep me up to date on their project, results, career), by email, dropping into my office, arrange meetings. Will come to me to discuss scientific papers or technical problems, discusses ideas for experiments, new directions"

"The key is that the postdoc is proactive, has ideas, is willing to talk to people BUT will always discuss things with the [PI] and be willing to exchange ideas and allow the [PI] to modify or influence. A good relationship is built on meetings with the [PI] that have real scientific content and discussion rather than simply a business meeting or a list of problems."

*   Are you surprised about what has been written? If yes, which parts?
*   Do you understand why these comments have been made?
*   Thinking about your own behaviours and interactions with your PI, how would they describe you?
*   Does your PI value your contributions? If you don't know — why don't you?
*   If we were to ask your current PI "what they most value about you and your work and what they find most frustrating" what would they say?

Building a good relationship

In building a good relationship with your PI you will need to consider: your PI is your line manager, that you work for them, the success of the project will have a direct impact on their career and promotion opportunities, and that for a relationship to work effectively both sides have to be aware of the other person's needs. When postdocs who feel they have issues with their PI ask for our help, often we find that the underlying cause of the problems is a lack of appreciation of the other person's perspective. So, how can you avoid this situation? Ask! Clear and open communication is vital.

How can you establish good communication channels with your PI? If you are about to start a new postdoc, then you have the ideal opportunity to work out the parameters of this new relationship. Schedule a meeting to ask what you can expect from your PI, what they expect from you, and to clarify a schedule for future meetings. In light of this, what are you expecting from your PI and is it realistic? This meeting would also be the time to understand their communication preferences (email, face-to-face, phone). If you are well into your postdoc contract, there is nothing to stop you having a similar conversation; you could perhaps ask for a review of how the project is going and feedback on your work?

All PIs are busy, possibly stressed, and certainly juggling many balls in the air at once. Your best chance of building a good relationship with them is to make yourself easy to communicate with. Some of our top tips for this are:

- ☑ Set a short agenda by email before a meeting so that the PI knows what to expect.
- ☑ Give them plenty of time to read any related paperwork first.
- ☑ If there are problems come prepared to offer possible solutions to chat over (do NOT be the person who only brings problems to the table).
- ☑ Share your successes and interesting results. Do not cancel the meeting because everything is going fine.
- ☑ Always have your updated publication plan at the meeting.
- ☑ Ask for feedback (noting that the PI was appointed because they are excellent at research, not necessarily people skills).
- ☑ After each meeting confirm any actions by email and thank them for their time.

Take a proactive stance, do not wait to be asked. One postdoc we worked with stated that their PI had not given them an annual appraisal and they had been there 3 years. We asked if they had asked for one. "No" came the reply. Again, at the risk of sounding like a broken record, you are in charge of your career!

Bring solutions to your PI, not problems.

Keep your PI in the loop about training, conferences and ask about annual leave before you have booked it. If you are sick, let them know as they have a duty of care as your line manager. The AWOL (absent without leave) postdoc is the most frustrating for the PI — are they late/absent/at an interview? Think about the hours you spend at work — do you overlap sufficiently with your PI?

If your PI shares an open office with you think carefully about any unwanted messages your behaviour might send. You might be taking a five-minute break having worked all morning writing a paper but if your PI sees you on social media at that moment what impression do they have of you? Being professional is important in helping to build trust and respect of your colleagues (especially your PI). So, if you have earned a break, then take one away from your "work" screen. Take a walk and use your personal device for social media or calls. Use the downtime to boost your brain for the next task. Successful postdocs we have worked with seem to have a really good separation of work and personal — with time for both.

✳   How much time do you **honestly** spend on social media, news sites, surfing the web each day? You need to be honest with yourself — take a look at our time management section!

And, a final caveat would be: be cautious about being a "friend" to your PI on any social media (unless it is a work related stream in which case ensure you are separating work and personal with different accounts). Your boss may not want to see your posts of your cat/cakes/trip to Corfu ... unless, of course, your research is about cats and cakes in Corfu!

Conclusion

Postdocs are professional researchers. For many people it is their first "proper" job, but because it is in an academic setting it can make the break from student to professional harder. Building professional relationships (or even reframing them if you have stayed in the same institution) requires effort and planning. Think very carefully about the working relationship with your PI and they may be fantastic colleagues, referees, collaborators and connections for the rest of your life.

What every postdoc needs to know about ... the relationship with their PI

☑   Communicate early and often.
☑   Do not assume the quality of your work will speak for itself, be professional.
☑   The relationship is important. Make it work for you.

Resources

Many universities will have guidance on roles and responsibilities of PIs. Check your HR website.

Vitae has good sections for research staff available at https://www.vitae. ac.uk/doing-research/research-staff/practicalities-of-being-research-staff.

University and College Union (UCU) has a good researcher survival guide available at https://www.ucu.org.uk/researchersurvival.

Acas (Advisory, Conciliation and Arbitration Service) provides free and impartial information and advice to employers and employees on all aspects of workplace relations and employment law available at http://www.acas.org.uk/index.aspx?articleid=797.

UK Research Staff Association (UKRSA) provides a collective voice for researchers available at https://www.vitae.ac.uk/doing-research/research-staff/uk-research-staff-association.

Citizens advice gives free, confidential information and advice to assist people with money, legal, consumer and other problems available at https://www.citizensadvice.org.uk.

Chapter 6

Publish and Prosper

Write!

Researchers communicate all the time and the majority of this is through the written word. Just think of the variety of researcher writing: emails, reports, abstracts, reviews, blogs, experimental documentation, biographies, papers, press releases, applications for funding and jobs ... Given we write every day, why is writing for publication often a sticking point with many researchers?

Publication plans

You will need a strategy for publishing your work. Rightly or wrongly, one of the main ways that research and researchers are judged is through their published writing. In many disciplines, publishing in a peer-reviewed, high impact journal tends to be viewed most favourably. Therefore, you need to plan for when and where you would like to publish. Obviously, this is not completely within your control, and while you may *want* to publish in the top ranked journal in your field, you don't get to make that decision! Also, your plan will need to be revised and changed alongside the ups and downs of your research, but if you don't have a plan you can't change it — so, make sure you have a plan!

So, where to start? The first step is to take a good look at your project and work out the publications that could be generated from the research. All fields are different when it comes to the number and rate of publications but you should be opportunistic. For example, is there a technical note that can be published alongside the main findings? Could you write a review paper? The publication plan will obviously need to be drawn up involving your PI, and this is the time to hammer out who are the authors and in what order will they be listed.

You may well have publications still in progress from your PhD. If you want these to ever see the light of day they need to be timetabled into your week around your postdoc project i.e. straight away! We have lost count of the number of postdocs who, several years in, still claim to have some PhD papers "almost" ready. No paper counts until it is published.

An important part of the plan is to understand how long publishing takes for the journals you are aiming for. A publication plan should contain a submission date (which you have some control over) and allow time for review and revisions. If your future plans involve having those publications by a deadline (fellowship applications, grants or the Research Excellence Framework (REF) then this becomes even more important.

This overall, "big picture" publication plan will then need to be supplemented with managing writing and often coordinating multiple authors on each individual article. More plans! …but then you must put them into action.

"[It is] critical to understand the importance placed on different types and levels of publication in your field and how that will impact on future career progression e.g. reviews are good for profile but don't count against the REF for biomedical research and can be enormous time sinks so priority should be given to primary research publications."

James Harker

Putting the plan into action

So, once you have your plan where to start? Our advice would be "write right now"! Publishing is part of the postdoc role so make writing a part of every single work day. Some people can sit down and write for eight hours straight but research has shown that for most people a "daily snack" works much better than a monthly "feast" (see article: Want to publish more? Then train like an athlete. Tomorrow's Professor, **66**(1), 4 September 2012). A systematic approach is essential. So, pick your best time of day to write (when you are going to work well — for this author that is first thing in the morning), think about how long you can meaningfully write for (do not include the making a drink, checking emails/news and other "settling" behaviour!) and start those publications. There is always something you can write before the data starts to come in and the act of writing can often clarify one's thinking. If you are likely to be disturbed take yourself and a laptop away from the research setting or "advertise" that this is your writing time to your colleagues (big earphones can work well in an open plan office environment, both as an aid to reduce disturbing noises and as a visual cue that you don't want to be disturbed). Whichever you decide to do make sure you have turned off notifications from emails/social media so you can concentrate on the job in hand.

Some institutions have set up writing groups for those looking to boost their written output. These vary but most involve a set time each week where people will come together to write individually for a fixed time followed by a chance to peer review each other's work. This peer feedback can be very useful even if, and perhaps especially if, the reviewers are outside the discipline of the writer. Most institutions also offer support for those writing in English as a second language through personal development courses. In both cases you may have to hunt around for events as writing development can be hosted by libraries, postdoc associations, staff development, HR, student support…. If you cannot find a group, why not start one?

Tips for those lacking motivation to start/continue writing

☑ Do 10 mins. Once you have started something you may find that you can keep going.

☑ Break each section of writing into small achievable sections. For example, "write the introduction" can feel overwhelming. "Write the first paragraph of the introduction" seems more within our attention spans and, applying the rule above, will only take 10 mins ...and you will then potentially carry on, but even if you don't you will have written the first paragraph. It's a start!

☑ Don't wait for the motivation fairy (Kearns and Gardiner, 2011); Nature **472**(127). As this great article describes, she doesn't magically appear and put you in the mood for writing. You may never be "ready" i.e. have the perfect data, graph, pens, references ... you just have to start. We, the authors, are guilty of the seemingly useful activities "needed" before you can actually write anything. Indeed, when about to write a section about time management one of us (who shall remain anonymous) spent a long period of time (that was allocated for writing this section) performing internet searches on this topic. This anonymous author then got side-tracked by the advice that "a tidy desk helps productivity" and proceeded to spend another half an hour in tidying up the offensively untidy desk. The result? A tidy desk, no writing, and a profound sense of irony mixed with guilt! You have been warned!!

☑ Write the first sentence of the next thing you need to tackle. This way you have already started and it is then easier to continue, e.g. if you finish writing the introduction and are moving on to the discussion the following day, then write the first sentence of the discussion before closing down the computer for the night.

☑ Try the Pomodoro technique. Small bursts of focused, uninterrupted activity can lead to greater progression.

☑ Give yourself a reward when you have finished what you wanted to achieve in a set time. Your reward might be to look at social media, make a cup of tea, go for a walk ... we vote for cake!

With only 455 words to go, the slice of cake reward edged closer.

☑ Try some free-writing exercises — switch off your "internal editor" and using a pen or pencil just write whatever comes into your mind about the topic you are trying to write on. Do this for 7 mins without stopping, correcting, or concern for grammar or punctuation. Don't worry, nobody else will see it! You can then move on to generative writing where you will pick something from your free writing and write solidly for a set period e.g. 5 mins with a view that someone else will read it.

☑ Externalise your deadlines. Let someone know that you will get a draft to them by a certain time, for example. Or get someone to nag you — a friend, a colleague, your mum ... you will want to get the writing done just to stop them pestering you!

☑ Get an app. There are various ones available with different types of motivation: rewards e.g. a cartoon cat that you "earn" after writing a set amount of words, or punishment e.g. deleting all your work if you don't write the set amount of words in a certain time frame!

Feedback

Once you have a draft it is time to get feedback. Start with yourself. After a break from the manuscript (when you could be writing the next!) re-read your work. Thinking of it as a whole, does it flow? Does it say what you want it to? Redraft at this level and then move onto the more detailed changes. It will then be time to solicit other people's views. Choose your advisors well — it may well not be appropriate to show a rough draft to your PI. When asking people to review your work think about the following:

- ☑ Give them enough to read (not just draft bullet point ideas).
- ☑ Don't overwhelm them.
- ☑ Give them enough time.
- ☑ Ask for specific feedback (English use, statistics, literature review, etc.).
- ☑ Have a variety of advisors.
- ☑ Be open to advice and weigh it up.
- ☑ Ask them what format they would like to read best (e.g. printed out or electronic version).
- ☑ Have a member of the target audience giving you feedback.

Creating a publication ready for submission is likely to take several iterations of review and redrafting by you and the other authors. But for the perfectionists amongst you we would like to remind you of the adage, "There is the perfect paper and then there is the paper that is submitted." Make sure at least one of the authors can call time on it and send it off!

Writing excellent manuscripts

The number one tip is to write a good title. It is the only thing that you can guarantee people will read. If the title does not describe the essence of your work, if it is overly complicated, full of jargon, or annoyingly witty in its use of acronyms, then potential readers (and citers) may not bother to read any more. The same holds true for the abstract of journal articles, which is the second thing that most readers will glance through before investing time in reading the full article. Obviously, the full article then has to be well written. The *Lancet* summarises that they are looking for: "Any original contribution that advances or illuminates medical science or practice, or that educates or entertains the journal's readers." While entertainment may not be the first thing that springs to mind when you are asked about writing research articles, if you can achieve that through describing your research findings you are onto a winner! So, how can you write an informative and entertaining article? Here are some concepts to think about.

Clarity and coherence

Remove jargon wherever possible and don't *utilise* words with an "ise" on the end when you could *use* a simpler word! (Do you see what we did there? OK it wasn't that clever, but you get the idea!) It is actually relatively easy to make the work you do sound complex (because it usually is), but it is much more difficult to describe your research findings well using simple language. Certainly in the case of journals, the higher impact publications tend to be for a broader audience; therefore, the level of acceptable jargon needs to be lower than for a specialist audience. The problem is that you are likely to be oblivious to the everyday jargon that creeps into your vocabulary so make sure you get someone from outside your team, discipline or area of expertise to give feedback, as appropriate.

Feedback is also highly valuable in helping to ensure that the manuscript "tells a story." We don't mean that you have made it up (!), but that the whole piece of work flows in terms of a logical sequence of events or thoughts. The best work to read does not take effort to follow what the authors are trying to say; the authors somehow guide you along through their work as though they are a tour guide. As researchers we often get so entwined with the details of the work that looking at the overall picture becomes more challenging, therefore making an outsider's view really useful.

Consistency and conciseness

For example: ise or ize? American and English spelling of words such as specialize or specialise should be done in line with the guidelines from the publication and consistently. (Please feel free to point out all the deliberate (honestly, they are deliberate) mistakes in this book!) Generally, acronyms and abbreviations should be described in full at the first use if to be used more than three times throughout the text and then the abbreviated version used consistently.

Conciseness might be a preoccupation in the sciences rather than the humanities, but word or character limits enforced for journal articles are realities that have to be embraced. In other (more concise) words, if a journal has a word limit — stick to it!

Knowing the publishing process

What gets accepted for publication in most journals is based on editorial input and the opinions of expert peer reviewers, although more open publishing platforms are becoming available online and with a drive to make research more openly available this trend is likely to both continue and evolve. It is important to check the author guidelines and the details of the review process for the journal you are submitting to. Common forms of peer review include: "single-blind" in which the reviewers will be given the names of the authors but the authors will not know who has reviewed their paper; "double-blind" in which neither reviewers' or authors' identities are revealed to each other; "open review" in which all names are shared; "post-publication open review" in which your article is published and readers can post their reviews or comments on it.

While most researchers see value in the peer review process, it is not perfect, and there is continued debate about its effectiveness in promoting publication of research that may be highly novel and therefore at odds with the accepted ways of thinking. There are also questions around bias and ethical issues. The views of researchers (authors, reviewers and editors) on the peer review process were explored in an international survey and focus groups by the publisher Taylor Francis. Their data show that most researchers believe that the peer review process improves their article, but there are concerns about regional and seniority bias when the author's identity is revealed, e.g. if you are a junior researcher from a group or geographical area that is not well known for research in the topic of your paper there may be a nega- tive bias towards your research. Furthermore, the findings high- light that in the real world, publication of articles by non-native English-speaking researchers is negatively impacted by language issues. Whilst we work in this imperfect system, you may then need to consider collaborating with more well-known researchers in your research topic and seeking help with aspects of written English and grammar, as appropriate.

> "Consider new open online publishing platforms (indexed) as APCs [article processing charges] are much lower"
>
> Bob Patton

The ups and downs

It's a huge cliché to say that research work is like a rollercoaster with ups and downs, but there truly are fabulous days when you find out your paper has been accepted to a high ranking journal, and days when your paper has been rejected …again … and you face having to re-write and reformat the whole thing … again… to send somewhere else (we speak from bitter experience). Perseverance and resilience are key whilst at the same time being realistic. It's a fine balance. Take heart from the fact that even Nobel Prize winners will have had papers rejected for publication, and find a mentor or experienced author who will give you a guiding hand in terms of aiming for the appropriate journal for your work.

Getting cited: Bibliometrics and Altmetrics

The main point of getting your work published is so that others can read it, marvel at it (hopefully), and build on it with further work. Academia is mildly obsessed with how we measure academic outputs and their impact, hence we enter the world of bibliometrics and altmetrics. There are likely to be experts at your institution who will give you a more thorough insight into this world (they are likely to be librarians so enter their realm offering biscuits and all will be well!), but here are some basics and what we think every postdoc needs to know:

Bibliometrics is a well-established quantitative approach for studying research outputs in the form of academic publications, mainly journal articles. Output in terms of number of publications, and the impact or influence of the publications on the research community are measured. As with all measures and statistics, bibliometric data need to be used appropriately. Therefore, to make comparisons you will need to use normalised bibliometric indicators. You can't make direct comparisons using unnormalised bibliometric measures such as number of citations, h-indices, or Journal Impact Factors because you are not comparing like with like.

Currently there are three different bibliometrics systems that researchers can use: Web of Science, Scopus and Google Scholar. Please be aware that each of these systems uses a different set of publications, which means that the results derived from each may differ. While many researchers find that they get better metrics from Google Scholar, formal comparisons always use Web of Science or Scopus because of the managed metadata that they use.

Altmetrics, or *alternative metrics*, generally measure online material such as research blogs, datasets, or software. Data such as numbers of tweets, visits to a webpage, clicks, or downloads can be quantified and used to assess research. Online tools for examining altmetrics are available and this area is rapidly developing. ImpactStory and altmetric.com both collate altmetric information to allow you to examine the impact of research.

Sharing and promoting your research both with academic colleagues and wider society is hugely influential in enhancing your academic impact. In addition to the traditional academic routes of presenting at conferences, you can do many simple things to promote your research. For example, add a link to your latest research work in the signature strip of your emails, send your latest research paper to your colleagues, get your work publicised through the university's media team, give presentations at Research Festivals, write or add comments/posts to a blog, write an article for publications such as The Conversation, give talks at local charity or interest groups, even chat to people on the bus (don't try this on the London Underground though). There are also specific online research communities such as ResearchGate and Academia. edu which are aimed primarily at helping researchers create academic impact through sharing their research with others. Additionally, social media such as Twitter, Facebook and LinkedIn, if used in the right way, can be highly effective ways to share your research, both with academic colleagues and wider society.

Making sure they know it was you!

One of the key things when dealing with bibliometrics and altmetrics is to ensure that all your work is attributed to you, and your institution will be anxious that it is correctly credited to them. Therefore, you should use the correct address for your institution and be consistent in the use of your name and any middle initials, for example.

Many researchers now sign up to get an ORCID number. This is a "digital identifier that distinguishes you from every other researcher." It can be used in manuscript and grant submissions and ensures that your work is recognised as yours. Indeed, many publishers and funders now recommend that authors have an ORCID number. If you haven't already got one, it's worth a look!

Your publication plans

* Sketch out (literally, if you like drawing) your publication plans.
* What are the things that get in the way of your writing?
* What techniques or strategies will you use to battle these?

Conclusion

> "Just like Strictly Come Dancing ... Keep on writing!"
>
> Nicola Ayers

Publications are a key success metric for researchers. For those who want to stay in academia they are essential. For those who want to move on into other careers they demonstrate great written communication skills, working with others and successfully bringing a project to a conclusion. Once published, ensure you use your network (see later chapter) to publicise your publishing achievement. The volume of publications in every discipline is vast and it is up to you to make every one count as a boost to your career.

What every postdoc needs to know about ... publishing

☑ It's important; so, have a plan and put it into action.
☑ Feedback is essential.
☑ Understand the system you are working within, including bibliometrics and altmetrics.

Resources

http://orcid.org/
https://theconversation.com/uk/
https://www.researchgate.net/
https://www.academia.edu/
https://www.linkedin.com/

https://en-gb.facebook.com/
https://twitter.com/
http://www.altmetric.com/
https://impactstory.org/
The Pomodoro Technique, available at http://pomodorotechnique.com/
http://authorservices.taylorandfrancis.com/peer-review-in-2015/
Waiting for the motivation fairy. Kearns and Gardiner (2011); *Nature* **472** (127).
Want to publish more? Then train like an athlete. *Tomorrow's Professor*, **66**(1), 4 September 2012.

Chapter 7

Teaching and Supervising

Introduction

"See one, do one, teach one" is the hopefully apocryphal method of passing on skills and knowledge in neurosurgery. As a postdoc you have skills and knowledge that will be useful to those around you. Communicating these is teaching! "Teaching" students therefore can cover a whole range of activities and does not simply mean delivering a lecture in front of 100 undergraduates in a tiered lecture theatre. Teaching can include supervising others, preparing and delivering lectures or tutorials, practical or experimental classes, problem-solving classes, e-learning courses or interactive workshops, seminars, building online materials, coaching, mentoring, or running a journal club or reading group. Your audience could be anything from school children participating in outreach activities to industrialists attending technical master classes.

If your career direction is towards a lectureship, you will undoubtedly need a good variety of teaching on your CV. All lectureship forms have detailed, perhaps daunting, sections on teaching to fill in; these can include a section on innovations and/or creativity in teaching, what impact your teaching had, course design, teaching methods, and assessment. You may also be asked to write a summary of your teaching philosophy. Some of you will be thinking, "Excuse me, my teaching *what*?" Your teaching philosophy is simply your approach to teaching and how you link educational and teaching theories with your teaching practice. Furthermore, many research funding applications now require you to include proposed public engagement activities, which could include elements of "teaching". If your career interests lie elsewhere, the great news is teaching is perhaps the ultimate transferable skill encompassing communication, problem solving, organisation and people skills. While teaching will not be an explicit or integral part of most postdoc contracts, you may want to get involved with teaching and supervising for a number of reasons.

∗   Think about your best teacher so far. What made them so good?

Why bother?

While you may ask yourself this question repeatedly when faced with 100 demanding first year undergraduates or a needy doctoral student, here are 10 suggestions for answering this question in a positive way!

(1) Gain some experience with your future career in mind — teaching evidence on your CV can be used for almost any future career.
(2) Some say that you only fully understand something if you can explain it to someone else, so teaching can help you with your own research.
(3) Take a break from your research.
(4) Develop your communication skills.
(5) Develop your patience.
(6) Share your love of your discipline with a (mostly) attentive audience.
(7) Provide an alternate avenue for your creativity and innovative approaches.

(8) Increase your visibility and profile within the team/ department/school.

(9) Inspire others.

(10) Is fun.

So what have you done so far and what could you do during this postdoc contract?

* Your teaching experience so far …
* Your reasons for wanting to teach …

Finding opportunities to teach

For some this is no problem; indeed, you may need to use your energy in demonstrating your assertiveness skills to say no rather than in seeking out opportunities. Some postdocs have teaching as part of their institutional contract. The latter is common in subjects that need laboratory demonstrators or tutors. This can be time consuming and it is always wise to check your contract.

For others, opportunities are less abundant. Speak with your Principal Investigator (PI) or the convenor of undergraduate or masters level courses that are run in your department. You could also get involved with skills development programmes or the graduate school who will often run workshops for doctoral students and will be delighted to have volunteers to help. You can make your own opportunities by setting up a journal club, or running a master class on a technique or topic that you are familiar with. Some other ideas (which may be dependent on the type of research institution you are working at) include:

☑ Look at the undergraduate courses on offer (most curricula are on university websites). What could you teach given your background? Again contact the convenor of the course. This is probably best done in the summer term (don't wait until

August!) before the new academic year commences (typically start of October for most British universities).

☑ Look at other local institutions who may well be looking for teachers (this would need to be out of your "own" time).

☑ Tutoring for senior school students ("A" levels taken at 18 and GCSEs taken at 16) could be a great way of working one-to-one. You could apply to an agency or advertise independently.

☑ Increasingly institutions and firms are looking to create online content such as massive open online courses (MOOCs) — your specialist knowledge could contribute effectively in this situation, as well as giving you experience of e-learning.

☑ Supervising final year undergraduate student projects.

☑ Supervising master's projects.

☑ Supervising PhD projects.

☑ Training technical staff.

Making teaching work for you

We have highlighted why you might want to teach, but the benefits of the experience really count when you are looking to the next stage in your career. How you present your teaching experience on your CV/application will vary depending on whether you are applying for an academic role or not. In academic jobs, the balance of teaching/research will vary associated with the particular job you are applying for. In all cases the skills (communication, problem solving, engagement, organisation …) associated with teaching should be prominent.

A tried and tested way to ensure that you are not scrambling around trying to remember what teaching you have done and finding the evidence to back this up (a vital part of all CVs — see our chapter on winning CVs), is to have a record of teaching. This can be digital or a paper folder with evidence in it. You need to keep records of who you taught, what, and when. Class sizes and class levels (e.g. undergraduate, masters). You also need to record feedback. Most institutions will have some form of student feedback for teaching and it is very reasonable for employers to ask for this. If there is no formal feedback, ask for some! Simple questionnaires (paper or online would work) or you can ask students face-to-face. Keep a record of any verbal feedback or particularly good scores (or average scores from a student who was struggling when you intervened). Alongside this, you should keep notes of particular techniques you used, innovations you implemented (very good interview material), how you coped with a range of students, etc.

If you are applying for an academic job, ensure you list your teaching and supervisory experience explicitly; do not assume people will know that teaching module ABC123 means that you designed and delivered three lectures and six tutorials, as well as setting and marking the associated exam questions for 75 first year biochemists. Do not use student names (unless explicitly asked for — we have never understood why employers want this information, do they care that you supervised a student called Ellen Patel or rather that you supervised a master's level project student in inorganic chemistry?). Anyway, (rant aside!), provide as many metrics as you can, e.g. numbers of students taught in different settings, the level of the student, the length of the project you supervised, feedback scores. It is important to note that while you might not be the official supervisor for a PhD student, for example, if you are supervising them on a day-to-day basis you can include this experience on your CV or application; just don't give yourself a title you don't have. The following list of sample questions asked at lecturer interviews will give you an idea of what evidence you will need to build up:

☐ What teaching experience have you had to date?
☐ How have you adapted your teaching to help your students?
☐ How would you describe your teaching philosophy?
☐ How could you bring your research into the teaching here?
☐ Please give us an example of a teaching activity that you think is particularly innovative?
☐ What do you find challenging about teaching?

Take time out to ponder your teaching philosophy.

Most universities will offer all new lecturers a "Certificate in Learning and Teaching" qualification that will be a required part of the probationary period unless already undertaken elsewhere. These courses tend to cover topics such as the philosophy and theories of teaching and learning, curriculum design, assessment, and a research project into a higher education based topic. You may be able to undertake this qualification as a postdoc which will give you a head start when embarking on a lectureship, and evidence of investment in your continuing professional development is valuable in all jobs. Check your institution's "Learning and Teaching Centre" or "Department for Higher Education" or professional development webpages to find out what is on offer.

∗ What teaching qualifications are open to you?

Most of the qualifications in teaching and learning offered to new lecturers at universities will be accredited by the Higher Education

Academy (HEA). By completing the accredited course at your institution you will be eligible to apply for fellowship of the HEA. There are differing levels of fellowship that depend on your level of knowledge and experience:

- Associate Fellow
- Fellow
- Senior Fellow
- Principal Fellow

HEA accreditation is awarded to programmes which link with the UK Professional Standards Framework (UKPSF). The UKPSF is a set of guidelines that describe the scope of professional practice required for teaching and learning support in UK Higher Education. It is a nationally-recognised framework for benchmarking success within Higher Education teaching and learning support. The UKPSF within teaching and learning support in UK higher education includes an outline of the:

☑ areas of activity undertaken by teachers and support staff,
☑ core knowledge needed to carry out those activities at the appropriate level,
☑ professional values that individuals performing these activities should exemplify.

✳ Look up the UKPSF. How does your experience map on to this framework?

Teaching is not all about preparing for academic jobs (or secondary school science teaching; although, the authors would like more PhD-qualified teachers in our schools please!). Teaching experience also demonstrates communication skills, people skills and problem-solving skills. It is therefore very useful when providing evidence of these for non-academic roles. When using teaching examples be sure to make your language clear. Words such as supervision, tuition, seminar, workshop will have different meanings to people in different contexts.

Teaching can be used to evidence many key transferable skills needed in all fields of work. These are often listed in the job description and will then be tested at interview. The following standard non-academic interview questions are where teaching could be used as evidence/an example:

What experience do you have communicating complex concepts?

If you have evidence of, for example, explaining quantum mechanics to first year undergraduates or gene rearrangement to high school students, you can formulate an excellent answer to this question. Just remember not to bombard the interviewer with quantum mechanics in your answer!

Give an example of a challenge that you rose to.

This could be a lab practical session for 100 first year medical students that needed redesigning, coordinating a lecture series, realising that all your students were struggling with a certain theory and designing an online problem-solving class ...

What are your strengths?

Communicating effectively with different audiences e.g. first year undergraduates in a tutorial session with, and senior professors in a specialist conference (gives a great spectrum of experience).

Give an example of a difficult situation and how you dealt with it.

We (the authors) have had a lot of these! One example is an experimental class where no-one got the expected results. This provided a great opportunity to dissect what went "wrong" and why — a great lesson in the reality of research work! A set of sample data was on hand as a back up. This demonstrates adaptability (see also question below) as well as preparation and foresight.

How adaptable are you?

Examples of having to explain things in different ways because you can see that the student is not understanding. Reflecting on your performance in a lecture, considering feedback, and changing things accordingly. Thinking on your feet in front of a roomful of students when the audio visual system does not work/the fire alarm drill messes up your planned schedule for teaching ...

If teaching really works for you.

If you love teaching it may well be an avenue into a whole new role. Senior school science and mathematics teachers with PhDs are excellent role models.

Some cautionary notes

Getting the balance right between your research work and teaching can be tricky. If you want to do some teaching in addition to your contracted research work you may need to negotiate this with your PI. How much you *could* do and *should* do will be dependent on many factors. Some factors that you should bear in mind include:

- ☑ You won't get paid any extra money (unlike doctoral students who may get paid for helping with lab classes for example).
- ☑ If you are preparing teaching material for the first time for e.g. a lecture this is likely to take around one day for each hour of delivery.
- ☑ Have you thought about how you will handle follow up questions and demands from students?
- ☑ Will you have office hours?
- ☑ How much help will you give?

Teaching will require you to get organised with materials, curriculae, past exam papers, etc. and there are hard deadlines which are in contrast to the fuzzy, ill-defined ones often associated with research work. This contrast can pose a challenge, especially when faced with a demanding student with a looming deadline for an assignment when you are trying to analyse some important data that does not have a strict deadline attached. Ask those who have done it before for tips and tricks. Think about when you want to be teaching (if you have a choice). Think about how to allocate your time effectively, and keep your golden time (when you work best) for things that you have identified as important for your career goals. This may mean advertising "office hours" for students.

If you are given responsibilities for the day-to-day supervision of a student (undergraduate, master's or doctoral level) then this can be a great opportunity. While postdocs often do not get any *formal* credit for helping students, this does not mean that you cannot describe the experience and the skills you have developed on your CV, but you cannot use a formal title for this work e.g. usually you could not claim that you were a PhD supervisor. If your postdoc is long enough it may be that the institution will consider you as a co-supervisor, but the rules for this vary and will be specific to your circumstances. Either way it is to your best advantage to work well with these students, not least because you are a fabulous human being and want to help, to mentor, and encourage more junior researchers (!), but also because they are potential future collaborators and they may generate interesting research outputs of which you will be a part. Please ensure you have a clear understanding of any authorships (if you are to be on the papers and what position in the author list) before starting. Remember that the academic world is small and students will move to other institutions; if they will speak well of you to other groups this can only help with enhancing your visibility and profile within your discipline.

Conclusion

Teaching brings with it some big challenges, but when you see a student have that "light bulb" moment the rewards are immense. We would encourage you to teach and supervise during your postdoc. And we leave this section with a thought to counter the "I'm not experienced enough to teach" feeling you may be having.

> "Public Engagement is a great way of gaining perspective on your research. Firstly you have to understand it well enough yourself to explain it to anyone. And secondly you will eventually get asked an innocent question that catches you completely by surprise and forces you to take a refreshing new look at your work."
>
> "Questions are always good — someone cared enough to listen."
>
> James Suckling

What every postdoc needs to know about ... teaching and supervision

- ☑ Teaching develops a range of skills useful in your current role and any future job.
- ☑ Think broadly and widely about the range of opportunities available to teach within your institution and beyond.
- ☑ Consider participating in courses and qualifications offered by your institution that are designed to enhance your understanding of teaching and educational theory and practice.

Resources

The Higher Education Academy provides resources and accreditation for University Teachers, available at https://www.heacademy.ac.uk and outlines the UKPSF, available at https://www.heacademy.ac.uk/recognition-accreditation/uk-professional-standards-framework-ukpsf

Researchers in Schools (RIS) is a teacher training and professional development programme exclusive to researchers who have completed a doctorate. Available at information http://www.researchersinschools.org

Science looked at postdocs teaching in this article, available at http://
www.sciencemag.org/careers/2006/05/postdoctoral-teaching-
savvy-career-move-or-distraction-research

WouldLikeToTeach is a website resource created to help doctoral researchers
and research staff find opportunities to get teaching experience in
Higher Education, available at http://www.wouldliketoteach.org/

Chapter 8

Transferable Skills Development and Taking Opportunities

What are transferable skills and why should I care about them?

A postdoc position is likely to be the time that you use highly specialised discipline-specific knowledge more than at any other point in your career, yet it is the more generic, transferable skills that you will need for the next steps in your career. Many of you now be frowning and questioning that, thinking with the critical, sceptical, cynical mind that makes postdocs fabulous, "I don't think that is completely true." Well, consider vice-chancellors and managing directors; they rely much more heavily on their communication and leadership skills than on their subject specialism and knowledge. While the frown may not have completely disappeared, you most likely see the point we are making. Therefore, as you consider your future options, those elusive transferable skills are important to consider.

Indeed, employers (academic, big industry, research based firms, government) view these skills as so important that the UK government commissioned a review by Sir Gareth Roberts (SET for success: The supply of people with science, technology, engineering and mathematics skills. April 2002) which highlighted the need for scientists, mathematicians and engineers to have transferable skills to enable them to use their technical skills to the benefit of

themselves, their employer and the nation. This had a profound impact on skills provision within higher education (HE) institutions for researchers. Funding was given via the research councils to institutions to develop skills enhancing programmes. These were initially aimed at PhD students and were then extended to postdocs. The programmes available at your institution will be part of this report's legacy. The skills employers are looking for form the basis of the Researcher Development Framework (RDF) and can be seen at the Vitae website (see Resources).

Why do we find transferable skills "elusive"? Because these are the skills that as a postdoc we often consider to be "obvious" or "nothing special"; "surely everyone has those skills so they are not worth mentioning." Or they are called "soft" skills which isn't very appealing. So, what are *your* transferable skills?

This is where most postdocs struggle. You are likely to find talking about your research project and technical skills very easy (you probably do every day), but most postdocs are completely oblivious of the vast wealth of skills, achievements, experience and expertise they possess. One way to tackle this is to sit for 10 mins and write down all the things that you do as a researcher. Think of a typical day or week (if there is such a thing!) or think of last week; what did you do? Team meeting, liaise with a representative for a supplier of laboratory consumables, analyse a batch of data, deliver a seminar, help a colleague with a piece of equipment, store and access large data sets, organise a team social activity, "look after" a master's student, attend a departmental talk, plan a publication …?

> "Think about your overall skills (including research) and not just your research topic. It is good to be passionate about your research but being aware of your skills will allow you to open new research and other opportunities."
>
> Marcela Acuna — Rivera
>
> "It's not what you do in your office that gets you on in academia, the research has to be good but the extras get you the next step."
>
> Sam Hopkins

∗ Set your timer and make a list. Remember to think broadly and widely and not just about the technical aspects of your research and link them to a specific skill e.g. seminar organisation = communication skills/event management/networking

What skills do you have?

Hopefully that exercise has started to make you realise the huge amount of "stuff" you do! But, you are possibly still worried about whether your list matches what you "should" have on your list. See below for a checklist of skills that may help — this list is not exhaustive. Tick all those in the list below that are transferable skills you possess and add any further ones to the bottom of the list.

☐ Time management.
☐ Project management.

☐   Planning.
☐   Designing and delivering presentations.
☐   Problem solving.
☐   Trouble-shooting.
☐   Creativity.
☐   Adaptability.
☐   Flexibility.
☐   Summarising information.
☐   Data analyses.
☐   Searching the literature.
☐   Perseverance.
☐   Communicating with varied audiences.
☐   Communicating using different formats/media.
☐   Public engagement.
☐   Organising seminars.
☐   Teaching.
☐   Managing others.
☐   Leading a team.
☐   Working independently.
☐   Working as part of a team.
☐   Negotiating and persuading.
☐   Prioritising.
☐   Ability to work under pressure.
☐   Meeting deadlines.
☐   IT skills.
☐   Language skills.
☐   Confidence to make decisions.
☐   ....
☐   ....

∗   Now go back and write the evidence/example next to each one in a document.

Giving yourself time to think about this is highly valuable, and especially before you have a looming deadline to find an example for your CV or job application. By carrying out this exercise you will also be able to identify areas that you may want to enhance or develop further during your current postdoc position.

In our experience, postdocs are usually modest and underestimate their own skills and abilities. If you don't know what skills you have or you are struggling with this section — ask someone. In fact, even if you *do* have some ideas it is good to ask people who will give you honest and useful feedback about your strengths because we are often blind to our own assets. For example, you may be fabulous at explaining complex technical things in multiple different ways when the person you are talking to doesn't immediately understand something, but you may be oblivious to this.

∗ Record what others say you are good at.

Who can you ask to help? Friends, colleagues, university careers service or researcher development team …

What skills do you need?

Transferable skills are skills that you can use in multiple settings/roles, so they are not just important for your future career: they will help you enhance your effectiveness in your current role, and they are not confined to your day job, they will also help you manage your family and personal/leisure life.

Alex felt that at least paper writing built up one's typing speed.

In this chapter we have so far looked at what skills you have, but what skills do you need for your current role and future career? i.e. are there any gaps? And can you find out where these gaps lie? Here are some suggestions:

Talk to your Principal Investigator (PI) or line manager about your progress, skills and areas that you could enhance or develop. These discussions should ideally occur regularly throughout your contract, but if your research work tends to always dominate discussions then schedule a separate meeting to discuss your personal and career development. Most PIs will be happy to provide this guidance but may not instigate the meetings, therefore it is up to you to request them (have you listed proactivity as a skill?). Higher Education institutes in the UK should all have some form of annual appraisal or work review system in place for their staff members which includes postdocs. Appraisals tend to consider objectives for the next year as well as any professional development support or training that you may require; so, you should be having this conversation at least once a year! Again, if you have been a postdoc for longer than a year and haven't had an appraisal, don't sit there waiting to be asked. If for any reason the format of meetings with your PI does not lend itself to a useful discussion on skills, seek out someone you can have this conversation with — a mentor, a collaborator or a peer colleague.

Discipline-specific professional bodies or societies may have tools and information for their members on professional development (not a member? — consider it). For example, the Royal Society of Chemistry has a professional development system in which members can log-in to set their own goals and record their progress. Having an electronic record of professional development makes the process of applying for your next position much faster.

Another example is Vitae, which is an international programme that was previously funded by the UK Research Councils and Higher Education Funding Bodies but is now a membership organisation to which many universities subscribe. Vitae have developed the RDF which describes the knowledge, behaviours, personal qualities, skills and attributes that are expected of researchers at all levels. The RDF is summarised in a circular diagram of skills (details in the reference section at the end of this chapter) — a good reminder that postdocs become more rounded people than just their technical skills would suggest. There are various tools associated with the framework that will help you identify which skills you may want to develop. Vitae's information is available without subscription and their Twitter feed can be helpful.

Further sources of information include funding bodies such as the Research Councils, who will often set out the skills they expect the researchers they fund to possess. For example, EPSRC fellowships follow a person specification which describes the desired qualities, skills, experience, achievements and attributes expected of the researcher. Look at these details to get an idea of what skills you will need to demonstrate.

An obvious but under-used source of information are job adverts. Start looking at adverts within academia and other sectors. What skills are they looking for? In virtually every single job advert and further particulars we have seen they are looking for someone with "good communication skills." Other top choices for skills in job adverts include:

- team working,
- ability to work independently,
- organisation,
- flexibility,
- good time management,
- perseverance,
- motivation,
- meeting deadlines.

Look at adverts for the roles that you are considering. If you are unsure about your future direction, start with the scientific section of a big national newspaper's job section online (such as The Guardian). What skills are they seeking in the candidates? Treat them as a tick list — which can you tick off (with evidence) and which don't you have (are you sure?).

The careers service, staff development team, or researcher development programme (or equivalent) may have developed institution-specific materials and resources to help you plan and document your career and professional development. As a postdoc your training may fall into several categories (some student, some research, some staff) — make the most of everything the institution has to offer. "Training needs analysis" tools are common and are designed to help you review your skills and identify where you may need some training or support. Again take the opportunity to talk this through with someone. A good critical friend can often bring to light talents we either take for granted or cannot see for ourselves.

What skills do you want to develop?

Having done some self-reflection and analysis of the skills you have and which skills you may need to develop, you then have choices. Which skills do you want to capitalise upon e.g. if you are fabulous at writing, do you want to get involved with writing a blog or with more mainstream journalism such as *The Conversation*? Which skills are you lacking that you will need to tackle? For example are you avoiding presenting your work orally at conferences or at local seminars? If so, how can you address this? Are there courses available to you on presentation skills? Is there the opportunity to present in a supportive team meeting or departmental seminar before presenting to a wider audience? Have you thought about getting involved with delivering sessions for school children? There are often various schemes available to researchers through universities, and they help improve your communication skills immeasurably. Being able to explain your research to 13-year-old pupils who will ask all sorts of unusual but interesting questions can be brilliant fun too! Now, the first rule of planning is to have a plan; take some time to jot down a few thoughts and ideas about the skills you would like to develop and why.

∗   List the skills that you want to develop and why.

Next you will need to do some exploration and research into what opportunities you have to help develop these skills. Pick a top three from your list and write them below along with a dedicated date and time when you are going to find out more about how to improve them (the next section will give you some ideas). Don't forget to come back to the rest when you've found out about these three. Sorry to sound bossy and parent-like but vague plans and wish lists don't tend to work. If you consider the "person, project and place" aspects of your postdoc you would always carefully plan the project, as well as elements of your research environment (for example attending seminars), so we suggest doing the same for your personal development.

	Skill	Time and date
1		
2		
3		

How can I find opportunities to develop my transferable skills?

Your university or institution is likely to have a careers service, staff development team and/or researcher development programme or equivalent that will advertise opportunities relevant to postdocs. Make sure you sign up to any email alerts, social media feeds or check the website regularly. Workshops and events are usually free of charge to the participants and represent an investment in your continuing professional development that will pay off both in the short and longer term. There are usually multiple opportunities at the departmental level to get involved with committees, health and safety, first aid training, seminar organisation and other activities that will both enhance your CV, get your name known, and expose you to new experiences. You may also have the opportunity to join a mentoring scheme, either as a mentor or a mentee — both of which can help with your personal and professional development.

Professional bodies and societies have resources, events and opportunities available to members that you can investigate. Look out for opportunities such as the:

☑ Naturejobs Careers Expo.
☑ "I'm a scientist get me out of here!"
☑ Events at the science museums.
☑ British Science Festival.
☑ Royal Society of Chemistry Career Consultations.
☑ Institute of Mathematics Early Career Mathematicians.
☑ Royal Academy of Engineering events.
☑ Institute of Physics "I am a researcher" pages.
☑ Wellcome Trust.

Taking opportunities

There are two important aspects to this that, through our experience of being researchers and of working with researchers, are commonplace; firstly, ignoring opportunities because they "don't mean me." Have you ever ignored an email looking for volunteers to sit on a department committee or to take part in a leadership course or similar because you think there must be lots of more qualified/experienced/"better"/suitable people than me so I won't bother? Or you've ignored the invite to the departmental staff meeting because they probably don't really mean you, they probably only meant to invite lecturers and not postdoc staff? If that's you then start saying yes to things and getting involved. If the email was sent to you then take it as a genuine invite (unless of course they are inviting you to earn millions by sending them £200!)

Secondly, deciding *when* you are going to do these things. Once you have identified the skills you want to develop and found the opportunities it's all well and good having a plan but unless you give yourself a deadline or some sort of schedule for getting things done, 99 times out of 100 these things will remain on a "to-do" list of things that you would *like* to do but there will always be some-thing more urgent competing with them. Don't fall into the trap of working within other people's priorities all the time, allow yourself some time for things that are important for your career and profes-sional development. After having done some research into the opportunities, diarise them.

As experienced trainers, we would like to add the following dos and don'ts when you are signing up for training courses or development events.

DO

- ☑ Arrive in time for any registration/coffee time — it gives you a chance to network.
- ☑ Be prepared to wear a name badge, introduce yourself.
- ☑ Take part in the exercises the trainer suggests (there will be a reason and something to learn).
- ☑ Bring a notebook and pen.
- ☑ When booking, make sure you can make all the dates.
- ☑ When booking, make sure you understand what the course is about.
- ☑ Bring business cards.
- ☑ Make an effort to meet most people.
- ☑ Switch off your phone — this is *your* golden time.
- ☑ Be open to everyone's ideas and thoughts.

DON'T

- ☒ Cancel unless you absolutely have to — organise your time.
- ☒ Be late (especially for a time management course).
- ☒ Make a "nest" in your chair and avoid meeting others.
- ☒ Neglect to tell your PI that you are going on a course.
- ☒ Disappear at one of the breaks — you miss networking opportunities.
- ☒ Spend the whole day on your phone/tablet/laptop.
- ☒ Fail to read the enrolment criteria and try to attend a women/ fellowship applicants/non-native English speakers-only course if

you are not a woman/fellowship applicant/non-native English speaker (you would be surprised how often this happens … and, sorry, Yorkshire does not count as a non-native English speaker!).

Raising your profile and creating opportunities

Some researchers seem to have interesting opportunities and invitations thrust at them from all directions. This is not by chance. They have developed a presence or profile that is known to people, which then escalates. How do you start to raise your profile so that people notice you and ask you to do exciting stuff? Well, there are multiple ways to do this; here are a few suggestions ranging from the standard academic routes through to more unusual suggestions!

Publish — not only is it a measure of success for most academic careers, it is the way to get your name known among your peers. You will need to have some sort of publication plan and give publishing a high priority on your "to-do" list. Additionally, as well as journal articles you could include contributions to book chapters, more mainstream popular articles for blogs or for sites like *The Conversation*, and editorials, comments, or review style articles. See Chapter 6 for further information.

Get cited — getting your publications in the right place and open access are important. Investigate the repositories available through your university and professional societies. You will need to become familiar with your citation counts and H index and other bibliometrics available through tools such as Web of Science, Scopus, SciVal, Google Scholar …

Make sure your work is credited to you — Look into setting up an ORCID[1] number to make sure all your work is accredited correctly, and be consistent in the use of your name and initials, etc. Think through a strategy if you change your name (by marriage for example).

---

[1] Available at http://orcid.org.

Tell people about your work — this can be through multiple channels.

- **Social media** are becoming increasingly important in the academic world. Organisations such as ImpactStory, Altmetric, ResearchGate, Mendeley and Academia.edu are developing metrics to measure the impact that your research has via these channels. Have a strategy for social media use — what are you going to put out, when and who are you aiming at? What are you going to follow and interact with? What time limits are you going to give to this activity?
- **Present your work** at any given opportunity — departmental, local (your institution and city), national and international (hopefully somewhere exotic) meetings or conferences.
- Liaise with your university's marketing or communications team about **media coverage of your work.**

Review papers or join an editorial board for journals in your field.

Webpages — maintain and update your university web page. If you have other webpages (e.g. ResearchGate) keep these up to date and professional. Ask a friend to internet search you to find out where and what other people can find out about you.

Networking — a scary word for some, but this does not mean approaching the most eminent person in your field at an international conference and striking up a conversation about their latest research paper (although you can if you want to!) This is about getting involved. You do not have to be a flamboyant extrovert to be successful at networking (in fact quieter people often make excellent listeners — a key and overlooked skill). See the next chapter for more networking know-how.

Organise events or journal clubs/reading groups — gets you known as an active member of the department or team in which you are based.

Volunteer for committees — many departmental or university committees require a representative or "voice" for the researcher community and it is a great way to meet senior colleagues and learn about the inner workings of a higher education institution (HEI).

Join relevant societies or professional bodies, or take on a role such as a regional representative

Get involved with **policy work** through your professional body, society or by submitting evidence to Parliament or via the Parliamentary Office of Science and Technology (POST)

Get a mentor — many universities offer schemes although unofficial systems are equally useful. If you want help with networking and raising your profile, a mentor can potentially help you with this.

∗   List your ideas for how you will raise your profile and enhance your visibility

Conclusion

This chapter certainly could be read with "this seems like a lot of extra work" running through your head. It certainly isn't meant to! Most of these skills are built up day-to-day as part of postdoc life and our intention is to highlight what amazing people most postdocs become. If you are thoughtful and proactive in your choices you can be in the very best position to move forward to your next career step.

> "Man often becomes what he believes himself to be. If I keep on saying to myself that I cannot do a certain thing, it is possible that I may end by really becoming incapable of doing it. On the contrary, if I have the belief that I can do it, I shall surely acquire the capacity to do it even if I may not have it at the beginning."
>
> Mahatma Gandhi

What every postdoc needs to know about ... transferable skills development and taking opportunities

☑ Transferable skills are skills that you can use in multiple settings/roles (and not just something made up by trainers/staff development managers)

☑ Transferable skills are often undervalued, under-appreciated and called "soft" (not complimentary in a tough working environment). They are considered to be "obvious" or "nothing special" by postdocs and academics ... they are not. This is completely wrong. They are integral to your current role and permeate through all you do (even if that is invisibly). It is vital that they are made visible for securing a future job.

☑ Find out what skills you have, what skills you need and what skills you want to develop.

Resources

SET for success, http://www.hm-treasury.gov.uk/d/robertsreview_introch1.pdf

The Researcher Development Framework at Vitae, available at https://www.vitae.ac.uk/researchers-professional-development/about-the-vitae-researcher-development-framework

BBSRC's vision of postdoctoral skills, available at http://www.bbsrc.ac.uk/documents/vision-for-postdoctoral-researchers-pdf/

The Conversation, available at (http://theconversation.com/uk)

Science festivals, available at (http://www.britishsciencefestival.org/) or local events http://www.britishscienceassociation.org/uk-science-festivals-network

ImpactStory, available at www.impactstory.org

Altmetric, available at www.altmetric.com

ResearchGate, available at www.researchgate.net

Mendeley, available at www.mendeley.com

Academia.edu, available at www.academia.edu

Submitting evidence to Parliament, available at http://www.parliament.uk/get-involved/have-your-say/

Naturejobs Careers Expo, available at (http://www.nature.com/nature-jobs/career-expo/)

"I'm a scientist get me out of here!", available at (http://imascientist.org.uk/)

Science museum, available at (http://www.sciencemuseum.org.uk/)

ORCID numbers, available at http://orcid.org

Wellcome Trust, available at https://wellcome.ac.uk

Chapter 9

Essentials of Effective Networking

Introduction

Successful people are good at networking. Don't confuse being an extrovert or an introvert with whether you will be any good at networking. It's not about personality types but about developing a skill which means that you make connections with colleagues and the connection will be to the mutual benefit of both parties; not necessarily immediately, but will be an asset for future work. People don't work in isolation although they may work alone on projects. Effective and successful academics have collaborators, supervise students who move on to other institutions, postdocs who become colleagues. Postdocs who transition to other careers can access information from their networks and may well link back to their research colleagues. The value for effective networking can be seen in the job market. Many application forms ask for references from several people. If you have an effective network, these people could also be your referees and you can choose those who would be best placed to be asked about your suitability for a role.

What is networking? The Oxford English Dictionary definition is: *A group of people who exchange information and contacts for professional or social purposes.* Is it different whilst you are a postdoc? It may be easier now — you may have many opportunities to become widely networked. But do note that "work" is part of the word "network". You have to put the effort in and it is not a one-way relationship. You need to cultivate links, keep those current and do your best for the people in your network.

If at this point you are not convinced about the value of networking or the need to develop networking skills... then ask yourself the question: "Who knows about what I have achieved and what I can do?" If you can start to list people — you are already networking. If the list is blank — time to get started.

∗   List the ways networking can help you with your career goals.

The interesting thing about creating a network is that you never know where it might lead. A chat with a colleague could lead to meeting a new business partner. Someone putting your name forward could lead to a new research avenue. Networking could provide you with:

☑   Future employers.
☑   Future collaborators.
☑   Future referees.
☑   Future contacts at a different university.
☑   A mentor outside your close working colleagues.
☑   Future friends.

Think about this possible scenario:

You are coming to the end of your contract and there is unlikely to be any future funding in your current lab. You've seen a senior postdoc position at another university, which matches both your skills set and your area of expertise. The last conference you attended, the group leader from the other group presented a paper, which you found very interesting and inspiring but you did not ask a question at the question and answer session. The group leader, at coffee, came over to talk to your current Principal Investigator (PI). Your current PI did not introduce you and you moved away from the group having not introduced yourself to the group leader. The job details included the contact details of the

Networking is simply building relationships.

group leader for "informal enquiries". You did not make contact with them. You applied for the job, and did not get shortlisted. You didn't ask for feedback.

You can create a different scenario by networking (in italics):

You are coming to the end of your contract and there is unlikely to be any future funding in your current lab. You've seen a senior postdoc position at another university which matches both your skills set and your area of expertise *you know the group because you did your PhD with one of their postdocs and you've kept in touch via LinkedIn and meeting informally when you are in the same place*. The last conference you attended, the group leader from the other group presented a paper which you found very interesting and inspiring *although nervous you asked a question during the question and answer session. You said, "I'm x from y and I found your talk really interesting. What do you think the future potential of this work is?"* — The group leader, at coffee, came over to talk to your current PI. Your current PI did not introduce you so *you introduced yourself, gave the speaker a business card and asked if you could visit the lab. After the conference you emailed the group leader, repeating how interesting you found their work and asked if you could visit within the next month.* A few months later the job details included the contact details of the group leader for "informal enquiries." *You contacted the group leader after talking to your colleague and getting background information about the job and the lab so that you could ask sensible questions. You spoke to the group leader and received really useful background information on the post being advertised. You applied for the job, and got short listed. At the interview the chair of the panel who was also the group leader said it was good to meet you again and that he was very interested in the work that you do and how it could contribute to the work of his group. You were offered the job.*

Your network

The great thing is that no-one starts with a blank network. We, at the very least, have our immediate work colleagues. Tapping into their networks alone would provide you easily with hundreds of potential connections. But this is not a social media game of how many "friends" we can have. Your network should be genuine and any networking goals should be linked to your personal goals (career and social).

You should try to keep basic records of who is who. A simple note in an address entry could record where you first met, their interests, what you talked about… You can reconnect with someone next time by enquiring how that talk went or did they get the job they were going for. This builds rapport very quickly.

So, who have you connected with? Take a large piece of paper (A3 works best) and write your name in the middle. Now using a mind mapping approach (see end of chapter for information about mind mapping) start to draw your own network. Initial branches from "you" will be "work", "family", "friends". But then think widely: sport's teams, your children's friends' parents, collaborators, previous university contacts from your degree(s). Then look at your address book (probably electronic) — who else can you add?

Now you have an illustration of everyone who could assist you with your goals. Even if they cannot help directly they may know someone who can. Choose two of your goals (one career orientated and one to do with your immediate research). Circle and then list the people who you could approach. Add to the list how you are going to contact them and by when. An example from one of the authors is shown below. Names have been removed to protect the innocent and to highlight the variety of networks this one starting point can connect with.

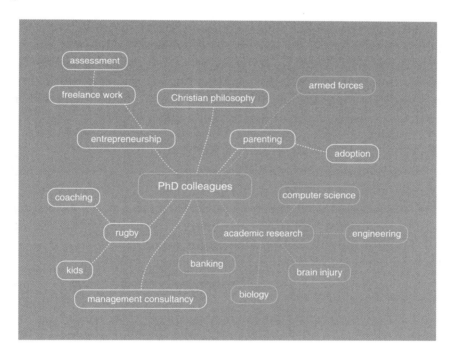

Challenges and fears — what are the blocks to you building an effective network?

If you find the thought of networking daunting, do not worry you are not alone. We have worked with many postdocs who find different aspects of this essential skill tricky. Some common concerns and our advice are outlined below.

⊠   I am too shy.

We would suggest setting yourself small steps to get used to networking situations. This could start as simply as just turning up to an event and then gradually setting yourself targets such as "talk to one new person." Asking a friend to come with you and introduce you to someone can be helpful. Have a good reason to network such as "I need a new job," "I want to work in their group," "I need to publicise my research." Luckily in the UK everyone talks about the weather so this can be a good opener (if you have the luck to be new to our climate — nothing special needs to have happened for the British to talk about the weather). The person who makes the first move to converse is perceived as confident. So speak first and they do not need to know how you feel inside. Also quiet people are usually great listeners. Being interested in someone is perceived by them as being interesting.

⊠   Why would x be interested in connecting with me?

If you have thought about why you want to talk to someone you should have your answer. If it is about research, put your research first and connect — it deserves publicising. If you are asking for advice then most people are genuinely helpful. In reality you do not know if they want to connect unless you ask. If they do not, then no harm is done. If they do, it opens up possibilities.

⊠   I don't see the point.

We have worked with many senior people and when listening to their stories what comes out is who they met along the way and how they reacted. In short, these people often have networking as their number one on a top 10 list of advice for junior colleagues.

⊠   They won't remember me.

We all have moments where we are not able to put a name to a face or think of the context where we met them. Help the person you are talking to by saying "Hello, I'm Sasha we met at the … You gave a talk about ...". Make sure you give contact details (business card) to them when you meet. Ensure you follow up the conversation by email again reminding them of what was discussed.

☒ I'm too junior.

Do you want to stay that way? If you have something worthwhile to ask then you should. But if you are genuinely star struck at the thought of meeting someone senior, could you network with their team?

☒ I don't have the time.

We are not suggesting you devote your working week to networking but some time does need investing in this. Making things double count (going to a seminar AND talking to some people) and setting aside some time each week to update your publicity (LinkedIn, web pages, blog, institution newsletters...). Gradually building up a network will certainly pay dividends when you are looking for your next post.

☒ I don't know how to set up a LinkedIn page.

We have picked LinkedIn but this could apply to any electronic publicity tool. Get some advice; you may be able to create the basics but how do you make it shine? Do some basic research and ask someone who has a really good example of what you are trying to achieve (networking!).

* Having read the tips on networking, what are your thoughts now and what are you going to do to improve your networking skills? Look at your institution's training schedule — many offer public engagement/outreach training which would include social media.
* What do you find most challenging about networking?
* What do you intend to do about it?

Networking arenas

Networking can happen anywhere but it is worth considering whether you have tapped into all the avenues relevant to you and your career. We list some here as an aid to you generating ideas that you can test out. If something does not work for you then stop, evaluate, and move onto something else. As a postdoc there are these opportunities:

Linked to your institution and research:

☑ Your colleagues (including your PI).
☑ Seminars and talks.
☑ Discipline specific forums (locally and online).
☑ Committees.
☑ Outreach events.
☑ Your research webpage/social media feed.
☑ Development events/coffee meetings.

Further afield but still research linked:

☑ Other universities.
☑ National societies.
☑ International societies.
☑ Interdisciplinary forums.
☑ Conferences.
☑ Special interest groups.

Local to you but not research linked:

☑ Professional networking groups.
☑ Alumni groups (school, university).
☑ Sports teams.
☑ Parents/carers.
☑ Social media.

If you find yourself thinking "I want to talk to others who are interested in X" and nothing exists, why not start something? Creating a group (face-to-face or virtually) is possibly easier than ever with the use of web based event tools and, as the organiser, you would be able to network with senior people by way of asking them to speak or contribute.

A note to those new to the UK. British people are typically reserved on public transport and you can expect the whole bus or train carriage to look shocked if you start a conversation with a stranger! However, we are very polite so will probably reply.

Top tips for networking at conferences & meetings

Conferences or meetings are fantastic opportunities for you to network, to inform people of what you do and to make connections, but if you are shy they can be nerve-wracking. Follow our top tips to be effective at networking at these important events.

- ☑ Pre-conference preparation. Look at the participants list and identify the people who you would like to meet and why, i.e. are they: Doing interesting work related to your research area? Based at a university you would like to work in? A really inspirational speaker? Able to help with your career goals?
- ☑ Highlight their names and search for them on the internet so that you know what they look like. Most people can be found this way. Ask a friend to search for you on the internet — what comes up first? Other people might be looking to meet you so make sure it's professional!
- ☑ It's important to remember that it's the coffee breaks/tea breaks, lunch and dinner, which are the prime networking opportunities so do not stick with your friends and colleagues.
- ☑ Decide who it is essential for you to meet and find them. If you don't know what they look like, ask a colleague.
- ☑ Introductions. Again ask a colleague if they know the person you want to meet and ask if they would be willing to introduce you. If this is not possible but you have seen the person you want to speak to, introduce yourself.

☑ Even in this modern age it is still useful to have business cards. If you don't have the opportunity to speak for very long with the person you want to meet, give them your business card, take theirs (if they have them) and make sure you make contact as soon as possible.

☑ Don't absent yourself from the dinner! If there is someone you would like to talk to approach them before dinner and ask if you can sit with them/join them at their table. This does not work if they are the VIP guest speaker and sitting at the top table.

☑ Dress appropriately. If you want to be viewed as a student, wear jeans. If you want to be viewed as a serious professional, wear smart clothes.

☑ If you are really nervous — don't drink too much or choose something really messy to eat!

☑ After the conference, check your list. If there are people you didn't manage to meet up with but you know attended the conference, send them a follow up email saying "I'm sorry I didn't have the opportunity to meet with you but could I visit your institution …?"

∗ Prepare a plan of action for your next event.

Conclusion

The aim of this chapter has been to convince you of the value of networking and to give advice on how to do it successfully. It is a life skill which will lead to success. A final word on what to avoid… Remember that effective networking is a two-way process, not just what you want from someone else. What you don't want to happen is for the other person to feel "used". So applying the mantra, "thank everyone for everything" is a way to ensure this does not happen. A quick thank you email or the highly undervalued handwritten note keep the contact alive and let people know you appreciate them.

What every postdoc needs to know about ... networking

- ☑ Ask yourself what do you need to know and who knows it.
- ☑ Always have a business card with you.
- ☑ Thank everyone, for everything.

Resources

http://www.researchgate.net

http://www.jobs.ac.uk/careers-advice/working-in-higher-education/573/how-to-develop-successful-networking-skills-in-academia

https://www.academics.com/science/networking_for_a_successful_career_in_academia_30577.html

https://livingacademically.wordpress.com/2013/02/11/10-networking-tips-for-academics-who-hate-networking/

http://blog.impactstory.org/linkedin-networking/

http://www.tonybuzan.com/about/mind-mapping/

Chapter 10

Unpredictable Research — Balancing Risk and Reward

Introduction

If research was easy and predictable, would you be doing it? Scientific research is exciting *because* it is challenging and unpredictable. Research does not flow smoothly. (If you think it does then skip to Chapter 15!) The joy of data lining up along the predicted curve is often tempered with a line of work screeching to a halt with negative results.

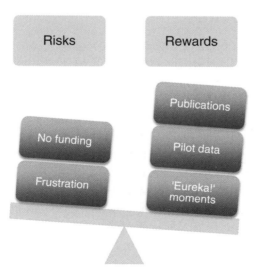

For many the postdoc years may be the first time we have really encountered risk with such high stakes. To get to the PhD stage you have often excelled at exams and tests from school onwards. During a PhD, given its training nature, those negative results can be built into the narrative of your thesis. Now, however, most postdocs are funded via grants with the future of any potential academic research career aligned to the success of past grants and with the early stage/pilot data generated for the next grant application. Add in external research measures such as the Research Excellence Framework (REF) in the UK with their defined metrics on what "success" in research looks like and suddenly we are starting to understand why the Principal Investigators of this world look harassed!

On failure:

"It may be the hardest resource to harness, but it is often the most valuable, precisely because it teaches you what you don't yet know and need to learn."

Jeffrey Bewkes, Chairman and CEO, Time Warner

Embracing "failures"

If we accept that negative results and "failures" are part of research life, how can we learn to deal with them? The literature on failure comes mostly from the business world. The start-up mantra of "fail fast, fail often" really doesn't apply to research. Or does it? If we adopt systems that review our work regularly then the warning signs might be found early on (fast). If we close off several research avenues through this methodology, then we fail often but may well find the right track sooner. It is the word "fail" that doesn't translate here. A negative result tells us something, we have pushed back the boundaries of knowledge. It may be hard to take, e.g. a potential cancer drug failing to make an impact on a clinical trial, or months of coding resulting in a simulation that doesn't match the facts, but it is learning none the less.

✳ What has been your biggest failure to date? What lessons did you learn?

Postdocs should learn to embrace failures — they are great learning experiences.

You may now be thinking this positive mindset is all very well, but what do I actually do when I see that my research project is failing? In the words of "The Hitchhikers Guide to the Galaxy" — DON'T PANIC![1] The following checklist should be used as a starting point;

☑ Take a step back.
☑ Review what has happened.
☑ Get someone else to review what has happened.
☑ Is it really a failure or just not the results you were hoping for?
☑ How long would it take to do the experiments again?
☑ What can be salvaged?
☑ What does this mean scientifically? Practically?
☑ Where are the opportunities?
☑ What lessons can be learnt?
☑ Ensure everything gets backed up.

---

[1] The Hitchhiker's Guide to the Galaxy. Douglas Adams. Ballantine Books; Reissue edition (November, 1995).

You have invested a great deal of time, energy and intellectual input into your research. If you are thinking things have failed, start by taking a step back. This may involve physically stepping back from the experimental wreckage (hopefully not!) but it is more likely to involve creating some time and space away from the research to get some perspective. Change venue, go for a walk, or exercise to clear your head. If others are involved then timetable a meeting so that you, and they, have time to think and regroup before it. If people's feelings are running high, this is especially valuable. Acknowledge what they are going through but give everyone a chance to calm down. If you are supporting someone, for example a distraught master's student, ensure they are okay. Talk them through when and how you are going to discuss the issues.

Science that "failed"

Spencer Silver was trying to develop a superstrong adhesive for 3M laboratories in 1968. Instead, he had invented the opposite: an adhesive that stuck to objects but could be easily lifted off. Another colleague from a different department spotted the potential. Post-it notes were born.

In 1956 Wilson Greatbatch was working on creating a heart rhythm recording device at the University of Buffalo. When he used an incorrect resistor value his device sounded like the human heart. He was reminded of conversations other scientists about whether an electrical stimulation could make up for a breakdown in the heart's natural beats [sic.]. His new small pacemaker replaced machines as big as televisions.

For others see Brilliant Blunders: From Darwin to Einstein — Colossal Mistakes by Great Scientists That Changed Our Understanding of Life and the Universe by Mario Livio.

Having created a bit of breathing space, it is time to review exactly what has happened. Channelling your rational researcher self at this point is important. Create a timeline of facts, not opinions, from your perspective. Write down exactly what you know (and perhaps questions to ask for those things you don't). At this stage it may be helpful to get someone else involved who is familiar with the work (but not directly involved) so that they can ask helpful questions. Describe what has happened and ask them to listen whilst asking questions that help clarify your thinking without imposing judgments. Is the only person you can discuss this with your PI? Continue your thinking and documenting (writing it down is the key to clarity) through the following stages so that you can present a more complete picture. No manager likes being presented with problems. If you can present what has happened with some routes forward then you are already working through the problem for both parties.

So, what is salvageable? Take a look at what you actually have in terms of data, results, equipment, samples depending on the type of failure. Has the project really failed or is it that the results are not what you had hoped for and this then may be the opportunity to readjust the deliverables of the project? Are there some quick steps you can take that will stop any further issues? This set back will almost certainly put the brakes on this part of your project but are there other projects that can be run whilst you regroup? Time is almost certainly one of your most precious commodities given the fixed-term nature of the postdoc. Some selfish thinking in terms of what would be best for your career as well as the project is important. Equally are there some strands of research that should now be paused in light of this event?

Understanding what this failure means scientifically may well take longer (hence the importance of the salvage step). A negative result may well indicate that a change in thinking is needed, a further review of the literature is required or that the methodology was faulty. All are areas where knowledge can be added to. This needs thorough and careful thought so discussions need to take place once things have settled down.

Practical considerations need to be thought of too. What does this mean for your publication plan? Does this indeed generate papers? It may be that the dream of a high impact paper has gone but there are still ways that results can be communicated: letters to the editor, short "note" publications, building your results into another publication or meta-analysis. What impact will this have on the grant? Do you need to ask for an extension given extenuating circumstances? If students are involved you will need to encourage them to make the best of events whilst ensuring they are keeping their degree authorities informed, if necessary.

Emma's experience

During my PhD we were collaborating with a large pharmaceutical company. We both brought different things to the experiment. Us: technical imaging expertise. Them: a model of disease. We were trying to image the effects of the model. The science was new and the imaging novel but we thought it should be possible to "see" using our technique what they had witnessed in their laboratory. There followed months of very hard work, long conversations and stressful reworking of experiments. Then one day it worked. It was a great day, tempered only by the discovery that on that day they had decided to simply replicate their in-house laboratory method. All those previous months they had been using a "special method" they had devised for us. We were at last comparing like for like and could visualise the results.

What did I learn? That science is hard work but experiments get better through "failure". And that clear communication between people working in different areas is essential.

The next step is to seize the failure and turn it about face. What opportunities does this offer? Again it might be hard to switch to the more positive mindset but this natural pause in scientific output could be a great time to take stock and think *creatively* about the future direction of your research. Again enlisting the help of colleagues may well be helpful. Or you could ask postdocs from other areas to form a group for a day of creative thinking about each other's research. There are many methods for enhancing creativity but some basics include:

☑ getting some space between you and your research i.e. moving to a different physical environment to help trigger different thought processes (so don't try to do this in your lab),

- ☑ using brainstorming techniques to have an initial "anything" goes stage (suspend the rational, questioning researcher at this point!),
- ☑ prompt brainstorming using random words or pictures to get you out of a negative thought spiral,
- ☑ look at different perspectives — ask other disciplines or use a Six Thinking hats lateral thinking approach (de Bono),
- ☑ swap "mode" to get thinking differently (if you are normally computer based use pencils and paper, draw if you normally write),
- ☑ use materials such as sticky notes to allow for ideas to be moved around/linked together,
- ☑ set some ground rules to create a "safe" thinking space (such as "no such thing as a silly idea", "everyone to take a turn to input", …),
- ☑ stick to a timetable that includes time for idea evaluation and action setting (to ensure everyone leaves with something "concrete").

Learning from failure may sound somewhat of a cliché but is very important in research. After all you are in the knowledge business. When looking at lessons to be learnt don't beat yourself up with "ifs and buts" but document factual lessons that will help going forward. One way to capture all the possible developments is to create a table of categories which cover every aspect of the project. Learning may well then arise that is only tangentially linked to the failure in hand but may well be useful none the less. For instance, if we took an example of a brain imaging study working with patients and volunteers our table of factors influencing the study might well look like:

Patient Liaison	Patient Preparation	Imaging Technique	Analysis Technique
Volunteer Liaison	Volunteer Preparation	Clinical Issues	Timings
Publication Plan	Grant Funding	Students	Literature
Data Storage	Tests Performed		

This map of all areas is useful as we can look at improving all things. The actual area of "failure" might have been a lack of patients exhibiting the sought combination of pathologies but seeing the table might prompt us to highlight other lessons (could include the difficulty of recruiting volunteers in the summer time). A wide range of inputs from people involved can be very helpful at this stage providing people are not wanting to ascribe "blame." Obviously this type of evaluation step would be very useful for every project not just problematic ones.

* What evaluation strategies do you use? What would be a timely method to do this?

Finally, do not destroy data or bin laboratory note books even if it all seems useless. What would have happened if Alexander Fleming had put the petri dish with penicillin in the bin (he was certainly throwing all the rest of the "failed" experiments away)? Ensure you know where and what everything is even if you have come to a halt. The great thing about science is that we do not know if somewhere a pivotal discovery is about to change everything we currently hold to be true.

Plan B (not the English hip hop recording artist!)

Plan A will be working hard on the topic you are grant funded to develop. You should also have a back-up plan i.e. Plan B. Consider extending further into the alphabet if your topic is a risky one! So, what is the Plan B?

Ideally, you should be able to develop a side project that is your own idea. The ability to "work creatively and autonomously" is a key feature of many job descriptions. A good PI should encourage this especially if it does not take time and resources away from the primary research. If your PI is not keen then you should try and cultivate some space to do this. Much can be accomplished with public data and a laptop in your own time.

How could you make this work in your field? Some good reasons for the Plan B:

- ☑ It demonstrates you can do independent research (thus avoiding the "Catch 22" of postdoc life that the next stage requires you can evidence independence but this stage necessarily involves working for someone).
- ☑ You have another avenue for possible publications (indeed this project should have a publication plan and not just be "pottering").
- ☑ Time spent working on other things often feeds positively into your primary project as it opens up lateral thinking and gives the brain some down time from a particular problem.

Other parts of this book link well to this topic, particularly Chapters 11 and 14.

Conclusion

Research is an exciting journey with many twists, turns, ups and downs. Being prepared for this as you enter your postdoc can help you build the tools you need to survive and be successful. You can build plans from day one that help, such as approaching your PI about a side project, getting to know other supportive researchers and constantly evaluating your research. The good news is that "failure" is just another data point.

What every postdoc needs to know about …
risk and reward

- ☑ If we could predict the outcomes with certainty, there would be no need to do the research in the first place!
- ☑ Unexpected results or failures can, on occasions, lead to unexpected positive outcomes.
- ☑ Get creative in thinking what you can do with what you have rather than dwelling on what might have been.

Resources

Fail Fast, Fail Often: How Losing Can Help You Win Ryan Babineaux & John Krumboltz 2014 Tarcher.

Rising Strong Brené Brown 2015 Vermillion.

http://jamesclear.com/failure-scientist.

https://www.vitae.ac.uk/doing-research/doing-a-doctorate/during-your-doctorate-the-middle-phase.

http://www.benchfly.com/blog/becoming-a-professor-how-to-follow-up-a-postdoc-fail/.

http://www.sciencemag.org/careers/features/2011/03/recovering-postdoc-mistakes.

Edward de Bono. *Six Thinking Hats* (1985) ISBN 0-316-17831-4.

Chapter 11

More Productivity, Less Stress: Relieving the Pressure

Introduction

We want you to get the most from your postdoc. As the previous chapter discussed, research can be risky. Postdoc life has its low points (experiments failing, papers being rejected). The Oxford English dictionary defines stress as, "A state of mental or emotional strain or tension resulting from adverse or demanding circumstances." A fixed-term contract is certainly a "demanding circumstance."

We all experience stress from time to time. "Good" stress can help us perform well. An adrenaline surge before we present a paper can enhance our performance. Too much prolonged stress can affect your physical and mental well-being. This chapter looks at the stress of moving to a new position and postdoc life. We also cover imposter syndrome, which is extremely common in high achievers (that is you!).

The stresses and strains of being new

A new postdoc position may bring the following changes:

☑ A new project to grasp.
☑ A new boss.

- ☑ New colleagues.
- ☑ A new research group/institution.
- ☑ A new city.
- ☑ A new country.
- ☑ A new culture.
- ☑ A new home.

The list could continue — food, currency, politics… This much change can be exhausting! Relocating takes you away from past support mechanisms (family, friends, peers). Settling into a new place takes a concerted effort. Some suggested actions to help you better manage this change can be found in Chapter 3.

It is also worth thinking about how change affects you. The work of Elisabeth Kubler-Ross in the 1960s provides us with a useful model to think about change. There are typically five stages (some models have more) with no fixed or equal timescale for each one. It may well be that people cycle through all the stages again with varying intensity of feeling. Some people who embrace change quickly may flit through the process. Others may dwell on a particular stage. Let's consider the example of moving institution:

Denial — You may not believe this is happening (even if it is a good thing — "This can't be happening to me"). Trying to maintain strong links to previous place without engaging in current location.

Anger/frustration — You may experience frustration at the new institution's systems/methods of working in relation to how you have done things in the past.

Bargaining — You may well try and bring some of your old methods of working into the new environment. Or may think "It is ok, I could go back if I …" or say constantly "in my old research group we used to do this …"

Depression — You realise that this change needs to be lived through. There may be a lack of self confidence and the feeling that you made a mistake in moving.

Acceptance after experimenting/deciding — You settle into the new environment having tried new things, made new friends and deciding on a course of action.

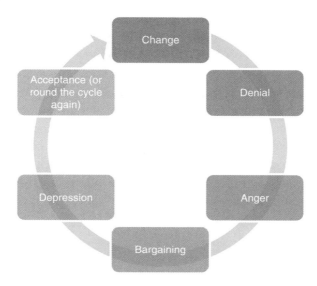

Of course, this may be over dramatising your situation! After all, people change research groups all the time. However, we often meet postdocs who have not given themselves enough credit for making big personal changes. The great thing about the internationalisation of research is that someone else will have been through this too. Often just a chat with a peer can help reframe things in a more positive light as they share how they coped. Indeed, many institutions are highly aware of the challenges postdocs face when starting a new post. There may be an organised mentoring scheme to help you with this transition phase. Once you have settled into your new working environment, you will be in the position to help newer incoming postdocs. So, the positive and negative aspects of your own experiences can be used productively to prepare resources or shape your advice for future postdocs.

∗ What big change have you experienced? What helped you through this? What didn't help?

The stresses and strains of everyday postdoc life

Being a postdoc can be a fantastic experience — being at the cutting edge of a research field and having a job that challenges you intellectually. There are, however, huge pressures to perform, to publish, to hit deadlines that will come in peaks and troughs during your contract, against the background anxiety of job insecurity.

How do people cope with the expectations of postdoc life? There are adaptive coping styles, which include active coping, planning, and positive reframing, which lead to improving the outcome for the person. Maladaptive coping strategies, such as denial, venting, and substance abuse, can lead to undesirable consequences. Our experience of postdocs who are stuck in "venting" mode (blaming the institution, blaming others, being angry at others for their situation) is that they find it very hard to move on.[1] After all if everything is someone else's fault then why act yourself to make things better?

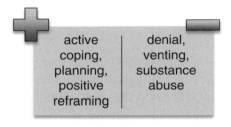

Taking steps yourself (with the help of your support network) is key to making the stresses on yourself more manageable. Some valuable practical lessons from postdocs we have worked with are:

☑ Take regular breaks away from the research environment.
☑ Take regular exercise (a simple lunchtime walk counts).
☑ Limit your working times — if you think you have to work 24/7 just pause and work out your hourly rate!
☑ Take on new challenges as an opportunity to shine, not an extra burden.

---

[1] Gloria, C. T. and Steinhardt, M. A. 2014. Relationships Among Positive Emotions, Coping, Resilience and Mental Health. *Stress and Health*. doi: 10.1002/smi.2589.

- ☑ Learn to say no more (combined with the point above helps the CV!).
- ☑ Set sensible specific, measurable, achievable, realistic and timely (SMART[2]) goals for yourself.
- ☑ If you have family responsibilities make time for them, be present (not clinging to a mobile email device) and enjoy that time (although the authors acknowledge helping kids with homework might not be the ultimate in enjoyment).
- ☑ Learn to delegate — small tasks to start with.
- ☑ Review your responsibilities regularly (do **you** have to run the tea rota, journal club, order the stationery and look at everyone's risk management forms?).
- ☑ Ask for help and advice.
- ☑ Find a mentor — they can be invaluable in giving you advice to help you through a stressful situation.
- ☑ Try to be proactive as well as reactive in your role.

On the latter point, a colleague shared the diagram below with us — a visual reminder that we should spread our attention whilst at work.[3] Certainly we should fight those fires (hopefully not literally) when they arise and keep up the day to day research. But without the focus on the "new" our research avenues will naturally dwindle.

---

[2] The SMART goals acronym has many definitions. Those used here are the ones that the authors find most useful.

[3] After John Adair's Action-Centred Leadership model, available at http://www.johnadair.co.uk via Ian Cunningham "What a manager does."

If you are feeling overwhelmed by stress, if it is affecting your sleep patterns or your health, or you cannot pin point what specifically is making you feel awful, then it is time to seek some professional help. Most institutions offer a confidential counselling service where you can talk to someone impartial and understanding. We guarantee you will not be the first postdoc to use their service. Studies of postdocs have shown they can experience high levels of stress (higher than the general public).[4] Your doctor (general practitioner, G.P.) or a private counsellor provide alternate sources of professional help.

What if you have made a career mistake?

You chose your postdoc position because the people, project and place all seemed perfect, but occasionally the promise and reality can be quite different. While it is important not to rush into a decision, it is important not to just accept things as they are. As a highly intelligent skilled researcher, you have an element of choice in where you work, and we suggest that you talk with someone about options and helping you with any particular challenges or pressures that you are struggling to manage. There is no one right way to deal with the situation that will work for everyone. However, ignoring things in the hope they will get better rarely works.

The fixed-term nature of the postdoc contracts works in your favour here. You have not stepped into a "job for life" and everyone will expect you to move on at some point. We can certainly point to parts of our careers that did not turn out quite as we had hoped. Ask yourself the following:

☑ What exactly is not right? People, project, place?
☑ What could make it better?

---

[4] Gloria, C.T. and Steinhardt, M.A. 2013 Flourishing, Languishing, and Depressed Postdoctoral Fellows: Differences in Stress, Anxiety and Depressive Symptoms, *Journal of Postdoctoral Affairs* Vol. 3, No. 1, August, available at www.postdocjournal.com.

☑ What do you control about the situation?
☑ Is it *this* postdoc or *being* a postdoc that isn't right?

The latter point may be hard to answer if this is your first postdoc. Time to plug into your network and find out what others' experiences are. If things really are not working out then explore your options (see the later chapters) whilst trying to make your time on this contract as successful and helpful as possible for you and your PI. Maintaining a good working relationship with your PI is especially important as you will need a reference from someone who may feel angry or let down.

Periods of success and promotion (your new postdoc job) can put pressure on you. It may be that you are suffering from Imposter Syndrome.

Imposter syndrome

What is it and why is it happening to me?

Do you feel it is by luck that you are working here? Were you in the right place at the right time to get this postdoc? Did your PI make a mistake when hiring you?

Imposter syndrome is a collection of feelings of inadequacy and can make you feel that you are a fraud. It can manifest itself as self doubt or feelings of intellectual fraudulence. It is most prevalent in high achievers, highly successful people.

The route from school to degree to PhD is one of academic excellence, surrounded by some of the brightest people in the world. It is a competitive route with examinations and a narrowing of your peer group as you specialise. You will have at least two degrees and are within the top $n\%$ (where n is pretty small) of people on the planet. If you have arrived by being a practitioner or a mature student you may well feel surrounded by much younger people. Add in family expectations and misunderstandings of the academic world, "So you are a researcher now — when do you get the Nobel prize?" We now have a fertile environment for brewing feelings of insecurity and inadequacy. It is no coincidence that the world's foremost universities highlight this in their counselling services.

> "Most people accept that there may be other people who have the syndrome, but think that, in their case, they genuinely are impostors." *Mindtools.com*
>
> "The experiences of students at Caltech, the values, expectations, and social environment at Caltech can be a fertile ground for imposter feelings." Caltech Counselling
>
> "The trouble with the world is that the stupid are cocksure and the intelligent are full of doubt," said Bertrand Russell.

Imposter syndrome is a spectrum of feelings. They may be felt all the time, only in certain situations, only partially expressed, or only felt when you are under pressure. It may be you do not have any of these feelings, but there is a good chance some of your colleagues are experiencing these. It is certainly something to bear in mind when mentoring students. Historically it has been associated with women but research has shown that these feelings are common in men too. The feelings include:

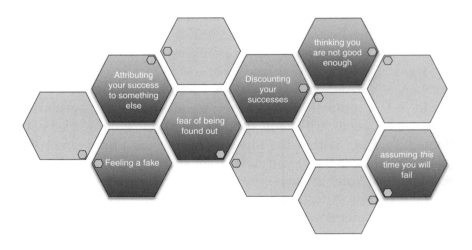

Being a high achiever and successful in research compounds the issue somewhat. You are always aware of the gaps in your knowledge because that is your job. Colleagues have information and know things you do not, especially in multidisciplinary teams. They are also your direct competition for time, money and promotion.

Imposter syndrome often strikes at times others would view as happy, such as a promotion or a pay rise. Changing roles into a new postdoc position is one of those times. You are jumping up a level from PhD, which was a studentship and so you did not feel that you should know everything. Even when moving to a different postdoc there are things to learn. Research is about the learning process and a comparison against others' work. We are taught to question, challenge and judge impartially about our research outputs. But we often judge ourselves, and other people, using the same techniques. When our perception of what is real stops being impartial or rational, we are stopping ourselves from reaching our full potential.

Imposter syndrome can stem from positive events such as promotion.

You may have the following specific concerns:

- ☑ Everyone else is here because they are great researchers and I'm not.
- ☑ I don't even know what is expected of me and what I need to do in this role.

☑ Everyone else's previous experience is more impressive/they have been to a highly prestigious university or collaborated with a fabulous team.

Work through the questions below quickly answering with your immediate reaction. There is obviously a personal line between being gracious and boastful but often we dismiss our personal hard won successes. Then think about how you could turn around your replies or your thinking to take control and ownership over your achievements.

∗ What do you say when someone congratulates you on being "brainy"?
∗ What do you say when someone congratulates you on giving a great presentation?
∗ What do you say when you receive great feedback from your students?
∗ What role do you feel that "luck" has played in your career?
∗ Why do you think your Principal Investigator (PI) appointed you?

Let's look at the facts ...

Some facts that all new postdocs (or even those who have been in post a while) should think about:

☑ Hiring a postdoc is expensive and a huge investment for the PI/research leader concerned. They have chosen you using a competitive process for a postdoc position that is becoming increasingly fierce.
☑ One way to combat the feelings of inadequacy is at the start of the project to have a very clear idea of the goals of the project and your part in it. Most of the work and activities can then be broken down into steps that you know.
☑ Look at the job description — you applied and won the role — you measure up.
☑ You won't be able to complete the project on day one.

☑ Look at key performance indicators (KPIs) for the role (these will be papers, supervision, presentations). Set yourself realistic goals: specific, measurable, achievable, realistic and timely (SMART[5]) and then measure yourself against these as you go along.

If you have stayed in the same research group, then you may still be in a student mindset or those around you might treat you as a student. It is up to you to be the professional staff researcher — simple things like keeping core hours, dressing more professionally, keeping (and allowing others access to) your professional diary will help with presenting yourself as a professional. If you behave in exactly the same ways as you did as a student, your long-term colleagues will treat you the same as they always have.

Whilst reading this list, if you have mentally generated some, "But that's not true in my case" statements. It is, however, true that making this postdoc contract successful for you will be easier with a clear plan of work and goals that are aligned both to the project aims and your personal aims to build up skills and experience.

Firstly, don't wait until you feel settled to get stuck in — you will feel more settled when you are actively engaging with everything this position has to offer you and have moved off the starting grid into the race. Setting yourself goals that are wider than the project is important. The 3Ps (person, place, project) can help here:

Person — what personal development do you want to have achieved by the end of this postdoc? Assessing your strengths and weaknesses objectively and setting on a course of personal development that harnesses your strengths, plugs essential gaps in your knowledge and provides strategies to moderate your weaknesses.

Place — what does your institution have to offer? Understanding the systems, opportunities and people breaks down barriers, and furthers your own development.

---

[5] The SMART goals acronym has many definitions. Those used here are the ones that the authors find most useful.

Project — develop an understanding of where your project fits into the whole: the group, the department, the institution and the field. You are part of a bigger picture; it is not possible to know everything, but relating your project to what is going on around you is very important.

The 3Ps help you generate a clear idea of what this postdoc is for: for you, your PI and the institution. Use the questions below to clarify your thinking. If you do not know what your PI or institution want, then now is the time to have a chat and clarify the goals. Clarification is important because quite often we hold ourselves to a higher standard than is necessary or even achievable.

* This postdoc would be successful for you if…
* This postdoc would be successful for your institution if…
* This postdoc would be successful for your PI if…

Some keys ways to combat imposter syndrome are:

☑ Acknowledge your feelings. This first step is very important — self awareness helps us to realise what is going on. The feelings are very real and present but may have slowly crept up on us or be so familiar they are part of the background and our everyday thinking.

☑ Counter negative thoughts with positive affirmations. Once we know our feelings are there we can start to catch ourselves in the act of a negative thought. Turning these around is no easy feat but stick to factual affirmations. For example, we look at a conference paper call and think "my paper won't be accepted, I'm not in that league and I'd be terrified to give a talk anyway." Turning that around "I will look at the past abstracts (gather facts) and decide if this is the best place for my work and if my paper is accepted I will give myself plenty of time to both prepare and practice my talk."

☑ Seek feedback and weigh it up realistically. If you have a good relationship with your PI then you can get feedback through periodic reviews. Further sources of feedback can be friends, peers or a mentor. Do not dismiss the good and dwell on the bad.

☑ Accept praise. This can be incredibly hard to do without introducing the "just" word. "I was just lucky", "just in the right place at the right time". But countering "just" (and its friend "only") is simple. Say thank you for the praise, smile and move on.

☑ Talk to others. Time and time again when we work with groups of postdocs they often say "I didn't realise we were all in the same situation." Everyone else is finding this a demanding role.

☑ Challenge automatic thoughts. These can sometimes pass us by without us noticing. A call for presentations (I can't talk well), a teaching opportunity (those students will all be brighter than me). Career progression in research is about seizing those opportunities. Stop the thought train and evaluate what the opportunity could give you.

☑ Avoid perfectionism — a perfect paper never gets submitted and yet plenty of papers get published. Yes, your data needs to be accurate and precise but it also needs to be communicated.

☑ Avoid perfectionism in preparing presentations. Spending a day preparing a presentation is probably a good use of your time. Spending the following five days fiddling with PowerPoint probably isn't!

Have a think about the following and note down your answers:

* Areas where I excel.
* My areas of expertise are: (minimum of 5).
* People say I am best at (ask, don't assume!).

If these feelings or others are causing undue stress then seeking support from friends and family may help. If you feel unable to talk to those who know you, most institutions have some form of counselling service where you can ask for confidential help. Often you can have a "pre-counselling" session to help decide if counselling is right for you. Counselling services in research institutes will be familiar with many types of problems encountered by their staff and the problem does not have to be a serious one to seek their help. Seeking counselling is about making a positive step to get the help you need.

A final word

If you are aiming for the perfect postdoc experience you are setting yourself up to fail before you even begin. There is no such thing. There are, however, many ways to make a postdoc successful for *yourself*. Those successes come from setting yourself goals that help you towards the next step. Those goals may be big, small, daily, hourly, career orientated, socially orientated … what matters is that they are yours and that once you meet a goal there is a small time to stop, pause and credit yourself for having achieved it.

What every postdoc needs to know about … increasing productivity and reducing stress

- ☑ Investigate and acknowledge the existence of Imposter Syndrome, if relevant.
- ☑ You do not have to be a superhero.
- ☑ Ask for help and advice.

Resources

Some simple stress advice from the APA, available at http://www.apa.org/helpcenter/manage-stress.aspx

Some thoughts on stress and the new research from University of California, available at http://www.ics.uci.edu/~jutts/WNARNewResearchers.pdf

Doran, G. T. (1981). *There's a S.M.A.R.T. way to write management's goals and objectives. Management Review (AMA FORUM)* **70** (11): 35–36.

Oliver Burkeman writes and broadcasts on imposter syndrome and other topics in an accessible way, available at http://www.oliverburkeman.com

Chapter 12

Diversity in Research

What is diversity?

We are all different and unless Principal Investigators (PIs) discover how to clone "perfect" postdocs, researchers are a varied bunch. Acknowledging and valuing individual differences is key to making the most of our resources whilst harnessing our common levels of high qualifications, passion for our research and drive to query the world around us.

Why is this section included in this book?

Academic research is an international endeavour with universities in the UK attracting researchers from around the world. Similarly, many UK researchers seize the opportunity to live and work in another country, giving research groups and departments a fabulous mixture of people. We are constantly inspired by the wealth of nationalities and cultures when working with postdoc groups, with a distinct shift towards internationalism in the past 10 years.

Nationality and cultural background are not the only characteristics of diversity that are represented in the researcher community. Researchers will vary in: *Religion and belief, sex, age, disability, gender reassignment, marriage and civil partnership, pregnancy and maternity, race, and sexual orientation;* characteristics that are all cited in the UK Equalities Act 2010. This reminds us that not only do we work with culturally diverse colleagues but that respect for all people is essential. This is reinforced by the UK law that states it is unlawful to discriminate against anyone with these protected characteristics.

On top of this, research teams may face the added dimensions of discipline-specific jargon or differing expectations of working practices. For example, the theoretical physicist who is collaborating with an experimental biologist and does not comprehend the complexity of "just" getting the cells to stay alive in an experiment! Differing expectations and understanding of how to supervise students is also a commonly encountered issue. Teaching in its many forms varies considerably across disciplines, across countries and the learning styles of both teachers and learners. This fabulous mixture of people, perspectives, and experiences brings a range of advantages and challenges.

What advantages and challenges do diverse research teams bring?

In the research teams we (the authors) work with, there are huge advantages as well as challenges in dealing with people who have different backgrounds and biases to ourselves. Largely, research requires a group effort and often this allows for some great advances. Even if your research is solitary, there will be others in your field who you will share your work with and learn from. One author has fond memories of the international cuisine at her laboratory... other more research oriented advantages are:

- ☑ Enhanced creativity.
- ☑ Fresh perspectives.
- ☑ Alternative methods/approaches.
- ☑ Greater insights into the world.
- ☑ Allowing individuals to fulfil their potential.
- ☑ Having assumptions challenged.
- ☑ Having clarity of communication.

∗ What have you gained from working with other researchers? What have you offered?

One researcher commented that working as a postdoc in the UK gave her a "huge opportunity to live abroad and to learn English."

Sometimes, however, there can be problems. These can range from little misunderstandings to serious misconduct.

- ☒ Miscommunication.
- ☒ Stereotyping and prejudice.
- ☒ Direct and indirect discrimination.
- ☒ Harassment.
- ☒ Undervaluing work because it does not comply with the majority of the lab.

* Have you experienced a diversity challenge? What did you learn?

The University of Westminster carried out some research about "Diversity in science, technology, engineering, maths and medicine (STEMM): establishing a business case," for the Royal Society's diversity programme "Leading the way: increasing diversity in the scientific workforce." (Wright, 2014). This report acknowledges that the business case is "complicated, subtle and highly contextual." However, the range of perspectives from a diverse rather than homogenous team, and the recruitment and retention of talent were seen as fundamentals of the business case for diversity in research. The report also highlights that business improvements were dependent on other factors including communication, as well as organisation and leadership of the team. The focus groups carried out as part of this research recognised that "ethnicity is seen in global, nationality terms rather than in UK-based minority ethnic terms," and that there is a "…general lack of visibility of ethnicity."

As a postdoc you may not be thinking about the business case for diversity when joining a diverse team! (although as a potential future manager this is something that you may want to consider more closely). Your immediate concerns are likely to be around working effectively with a range of different people. So, let's move on to consider this more closely.

Diversity in research enhances creativity and new ways of thinking.

Dealing with the challenges personally

So, what can a solitary postdoc do to acknowledge and value differences so everyone prospers? Sometimes the simplest of changes could mean the difference between inclusion and exclusion. Think about the following common (from the authors' experiences) research group scenarios — who could they affect, how could you change them?

- ☐ The research team meeting is held every Friday at 5 pm in the institution's social club bar.
- ☐ Two thirds of the research group came to the UK when the PI moved to the institution and they chat in their native language.
- ☐ The rota for equipment maintenance includes Saturday and Sunday mornings.
- ☐ Interviews for new researchers are conducted by the male PI and his longstanding male postdoc.
- ☐ Seminar slots are given to those who volunteer.
- ☐ The lab has an annual staff vs postgraduate football match.
- ☐ Access to the research group's office is via a mezzanine floor along a metal bridge.
- ☐ Everyone in the research group have to attend at least one conference a year.

Communication is vital in understanding another's viewpoint; don't just assume, ask. Observation of what is happening around you can provide insight — do the same people get to speak? Who is missing from group events? We all carry with us bias. The biases that we acknowledge we can perhaps tackle, but those that are unconscious are obviously going to be much harder. Many institutions now offer training in unconscious bias as part of recruitment or diversity training. It is the authors' experience that these events can often teach us much about ourselves as well as help us work better with our colleagues. Given your level of education and skills it is very possible you will be in a management position, academic or otherwise, in the future. Thinking about how you act and encourage others to act will be a key management tool.

The key to understanding unconscious bias is to start by acknowledging that we all have it regardless of how hard we try to treat everyone with dignity and respect. Our unconscious bias is deep seated and comes from the basic human tendency to categorise people. It is shaped by our upbringing, class, ethnicity, education, cultural context, and other aspects of our environment. Therefore, if we acknowledge that our communication with colleagues is driven by our unconscious bias it may help people to communicate more clearly. We see unconscious bias particularly in recruitment and selection. We will naturally be attracted to people who are most like us, and who we are most comfortable with. The danger of this is that we end up recruiting "mini-me's". Look at your own lab and the people in it. What are the similarities? Same background? Gender? Class? Ethnicity?

> People confident in their own objectivity may overestimate their invulnerability to bias.
>
> Eric Luis Uhlmann and Geoffrey L. Cohen

Dealing with the challenges institutionally

We can all help to contribute to an inclusive and productive working environment for everyone. In addition to the legislation and universities policies, there are specific initiatives and support in place to help address some of the challenges and biases of the workplace. These include Project Juno, Athena Swan, Stonewall, and the Race Equality Charter.

Project Juno and Athena Swan

Much of the focus in diversity in STEMM has been on the under-representation of women, especially in senior positions. In STEMM senior positions in the UK are still largely occupied by white men. The lack of role models and the predominant white male culture of senior management teams in higher education institutions (HEIs) means that junior researchers may question whether they would be welcomed to join the team and whether they would struggle to fit in. One early career researcher commented,

> "if I looked at the staff list, every single person looks like you [white, male — laughs] ...wouldn't prevent me, but certainly makes me wonder what the culture is like."
>
> "when the conversations in the lab are all around football, beer and rugby I feel as though I should either be quiet or join in. I don't feel that I can talk about my interests"

Project Juno and Athena Swan are two initiatives that have focused on gender. Their main purpose is not to promote women (positive discrimination is unlawful in the UK) but to encourage better practice in STEMM subjects for both women and men in order to provide a working environment in which everyone can achieve their full potential. The increased awareness that projects like this bring may also help to push at other diversity barriers. Project Juno is run by the Institute of Physics and specifically addresses the under-representation of women in physics at universities. In Roman mythology Juno was protector of women. There are five principles included within Project Juno:

1. A robust organisational framework to deliver equality of opportunity and reward.

2. Appointment and selection processes and procedures that encourage men and women to apply for academic posts at all levels.
3. Departmental structures and systems which support and encourage the career progression and promotion of all staff and enable men and women to progress and continue in their careers.
4. Departmental organisation, structure, management arrangements and culture that are open, inclusive and transparent and encourage the participation of all staff.
5. Flexible approaches and provisions that enable individuals, at all career and life stages, to optimise their contribution to their department, institution and to SET (Science, Engineering, Technology).

There are three levels of Juno awards:

Supporter
The department endorses the five principles and makes a commitment to work towards Practitioner and then Champion status.

Practitioner
The department demonstrates that its Juno journey is well underway. Qualitative and quantitative evidence is gathered and its initial action plan demonstrates how the department aims to achieve Champion status.

Champion
The department demonstrates that the five principles are embedded throughout the department. Further evidence is gathered and its action plan demonstrates how the department will continue to further good practice.

If you are working in Physics:

∗ Does your department hold a Juno award? Who is involved with putting together an application? Is this something that you could get involved with? (Not just women.)

The Athena SWAN Charter is run by the Equality Challenge Unit. It was established in 2005 for STEMM disciplines, and in 2015 has expanded to include arts, humanities, social sciences, business and law; the charter addresses gender equality in a broad sense.

The Athena SWAN charter process is based on 10 key principles to which institutions commit to adopting within their policies, practices, action plans and culture.

(1) We acknowledge that academia cannot reach its full potential unless it can benefit from the talents of all.

(2) We commit to advancing gender equality in academia, in particular addressing the loss of women across the career pipeline and the absence of women from senior academic, professional and support roles.

(3) We commit to addressing unequal gender representation across academic disciplines and professional and support functions. In this we recognise disciplinary differences including:

  • the relative under-representation of women in senior roles in arts, humanities, social sciences, business and law (AHSSBL),
  • the particularly high loss rate of women in STEMM.

(4) We commit to tackling the gender pay gap.

(5) We commit to removing the obstacles faced by women, in particular, at major points of career development and progression including the transition from PhD into a sustainable academic career.

(6) We commit to addressing the negative consequences of using short-term contracts for the retention and progression of staff in academia, particularly women.

(7) We commit to tackling the discriminatory treatment often experienced by trans people.

(8) We acknowledge that advancing gender equality demands commitment and action from all levels of the organisation and in particular active leadership from those in senior roles.

(9)   We commit to making and mainstreaming sustainable structural and cultural changes to advance gender equality, recognising that initiatives and actions that support individuals alone will not sufficiently advance equality.

(10)   All individuals have identities shaped by several different factors. We commit to considering the intersection of gender and other factors wherever possible.

There are three levels of award; bronze, silver and gold. There are institution and department versions available. These awards are increasingly becoming a requirement for funding from some sponsors.

∗   What level of Athena Swan award does your department and institution hold? Do you want to contribute to the Athena Swan work in your department by volunteering to join the self assessment team?

Race equality charter

In 2016, the Equality Challenge Unit opened the Race Equality Charter to all Higher Education Institutions. This charter aims to improve the "representation, progression and success of minority ethnic staff and students within higher education."

Stonewall

Groups and initiatives to support lesbian, gay, bi and trans (LGBT) people are available nationally e.g. Stonewall which has a Diversity Champions programme for employers. Most universities will have a group or groups that will provide guidance and support around diversity and equality for LGBT people. Examples include:

- Imperial 600.
- LGBT Equality Group at Surrey.

∗   What diversity support is available at your institution?

Mentoring and support programmes

We are all part of the rich and diverse culture of the place in which we work. Mentoring from someone else within your institution is one way in which you may help face particular personal challenges. Specific mentoring schemes may be in place e.g. for those returning from maternity leave, or joining a department. Transition points such as moving from PhD student to postdoc are often the times when extra support is required, and good employers will recognise this and provide help.

∗   What mentoring or support programmes are open to postdocs at your institution? How could you get involved?

Conclusion

As a postdoc, embracing the diverse group of people you will be working with will bring huge benefits both personally and to your research. Acknowledging this, as well as the associated challenges, is something that we think every postdoc *needs* to know.

What every postdoc needs to know about ... diversity in research

☑   There are many dimensions to the diverse research groups and academic teams you are likely to work in.
☑   We all have unconscious bias in the way we deal with people, acknowledging it and setting up ways to tackle it are key to overcoming these biases.
☑   There are laws, policies and initiatives to address some of the biases in the workplace.

Resources

Wright, A. M., Elisabeth; Snijders, Sylvia; Kumarappan, Leena; Williamson, Michele; Clarke, Linda; Urwin, Peter. 2014. Diversity in STEMM: establishing a business case. Report of research by the University of

Westminster for the Royal Society's diversity programme Leading the way: increasing diversity in the scientific workforce. Royal Society: University of Westminster http://wiseli.engr.wisc.edu/docs/Benefits_Challenges.pdf

The Equality Challenge Unit, available at www.ecu.ac.uk

Project Juno, available at http://www.iop.org/policy/diversity/initiatives/juno/index.html

Athena SWAN Charter is run by the Equality Challenge Unit, available at http://www.ecu.ac.uk/equality-charters/athena-swan/

Race Equality charter, available at http://www.ecu.ac.uk/equality-charters/race-equality-charter/

Stonewall, available at http://www.stonewall.org.uk/

Imperial 600, available at http://www3.imperial.ac.uk/equality/staffnetworksandcommittees/imperial600

LGBT Equality Group at Surrey, available at http://www.surrey.ac.uk/equalityanddiversity/about/groups/lgbt/

Chapter 13

Research Integrity and Ethics

Introduction

The research environment is based on a strong foundation of professionalism and integrity. Conducting research in a safe, responsible and ethical way, presenting data and publishing findings clearly and wholly, and being accountable to stakeholders all require researchers to be operating by the same rules.

Having completed a PhD you will be familiar with many of the issues involved with behaving ethically and with integrity. However, being a postdoc does bring with it extra responsibilities. You may be in a position to guide students or technical staff. You may be working on a variety of projects with different funders. Being a member of staff (as opposed to being a student) often changes your Intellectual Property (IP) rights. Being funded by industry may affect your opportunities to publish.

Use the checklist below to explore some potential areas where issues can arise. Your contract, research leader, institution's Human Resources (HR) department and university website will all provide information to help you.

☐ Who funds your research?
☐ Who owns the IP for the work you do as a postdoc?
☐ Is there/what is the authorship agreement on publications from the project?

☐ Are there limitations on publishing? If so, what are they?

☐ What permissions do you need to do your research? Ethical approval? COSSH[1] protocols? Home Office licence?

☐ Does your research need special security measures?

☐ Are you free to talk about your research?

☐ Are there groups opposed to the work you do?

☐ What responsibilities do you have for those around you?

☐ What protocols for research records and data management should you follow?

☐ How long do you need to store data for?

☐ What should you do if you suspect someone of scientific misconduct?

☐ How would you advise a PhD student about plagiarism?

Case Study

Cassia has been working closely with a PhD student on a project that has generated some exciting results. She has helped to plan and supervise the experiments and worked on the writing and editing with the student for whom this is a first paper. Cassia feels that she should be first author but the student feels that they should be first author given that it is "their" project. Additionally, their PI wishes a fellow postdoc researcher to be put on the paper to boost their publication record even though Cassia feels their input has been minimal.

How should Cassia resolve these authorship issues?

∗ What do you think will be the biggest ethical challenge with your research? What do you need to do/know now?

The list above glosses over a wealth of issues including using animals and humans in research, and how to handle clashes with your own personal ethics or morals, e.g. if you are anti-smoking, doing research which is funded by a tobacco company. Here,

---

[1] Control of Substances Hazardous to Health — UK health and safety regulations.

we will focus on four areas in which every postdoc is likely to have to deal with ethical issues to some degree: publishing, working relationships, data management, and copyright.

Publishing

Publish or perish! The phrase is often bandied around but publication (by which we refer in the main to scientific peer-reviewed publications) holds a surprising range of dilemmas. It is, perhaps, because it is a metric by which the scientific world judges the quality of its scientists that these issues arise frequently.

Common publication issues which have an ethical dimension include:

- list of authors on the paper and the position of authors within the author list,
- inclusion of all relevant data,
- declaration of any commercial interests (industrial sponsorship, etc.).

Most postdocs run into authorship problems at some point, usually surrounding arguments of input into the publication and thereby position in the authorship list (assuming it is not done alphabetically, which is done in a minority of scientific disciplines). You obviously want as many first author papers as possible as a postdoc and your Principal Investigator (PI) will be lining up for that "last author, boss of all they survey" slot at the end. Perhaps if papers only had two authors things would be simpler, but science is usually a group effort with postdocs and PhD students vying to avoid the middle ground in the author list. If we add in the terms "joint first author," and "corresponding author" it is amazing science actually gets published at all! On other occasions the PI might suggest adding authors whose contribution could be questioned. Journals are increasingly skeptical of the latter, with guidance that all authors must have made a significant contribution to the paper. The journal *Nature* highlights this in an editorial,[2] "We believe that we should go further in spelling out the responsibilities of co-authors, and in requiring an implicit acceptance of them."

So, how does a postdoc navigate this potential minefield? We offer some simple advice which works at the start of the project/piece of work contributing to a paper:

- ☑ Agree a publication plan with dates/journals at the start.
- ☑ Agree the authorship of those papers at the start.
- ☑ Agree a strategy for authorship should further papers arise.
- ☑ Agree a strategy should any of the authors leave.

This may seem like a daunting conversation to be having but demonstrating your commitment to publication at the outset and the associated timeframe shows you are serious and committed to the project. The timeframe is useful to avoid anyone "sitting on a paper" at a later date and should naturally tie into a research plan timetable. These should be in writing (an email to the relevant parties).

Agreement is especially important when those outside the immediate research group are involved. Collaboration with other institutions or commercial partners may need more formal agreements and may even prevent publication until after patents have been created (whose names are on the patent?).

Case Study

Jake joined a laboratory filling an 18 month contract which was vacated when another postdoc left the project. The PI is keen for the project's data to be published and wants Jake to write up the results so far and finish off outstanding experiments. The PI holds the data from the previous postdoc which will contribute to the papers. No mention of this postdoc in the authorship has been made.

How should Jake proceed?

---

[2] Available at http://www.nature.com/nature/journal/v458/n7242/full/4581078a.html.

Working relationships

The relationship with your PI is covered elsewhere in this book and is one of the most complex in academia. However, other relationships do require some mention in a section looking at professionalism and integrity.

Even the nicest postdoc in the world would struggle to get on well with everyone in their field and by the time you have factored in those who support your research in your institution, you have a large pool of people who interact with you even if your research is just you and your computer for the majority of the time. We will all be aware of the professors who "can't stand each other" and pick fights with each other's innocent research students when they present at conferences. The modern day postdoc works in a field which is truly global and this means "what goes around, comes around" is not just a saying.

Consider the following scenario. Two postdocs working in the same laboratory argue about authorship to the point where their working relationship breaks down. The research slows and fed up with the lack of publications one postdoc leaves the laboratory for another. Roll the clock forward 5 years and one of the postdocs is now working for a major funding body. They are sitting on a fellowship interview panel when they recognise a familiar name on the list of candidates…

Yes, it is true we have checks and balances in peer review, interview procedures and funding decisions but so much of academia is funnelled through informal networking channels — job openings, collaborative projects, senior role headhunting. The wise entrant to the postdoc world should tread very carefully and professionally. Your next reference will come from your current line manager (PI). We all have different boundaries for workplace relationships but thinking about the implications of these early on will make life easier and may even prevent serious employment/HR issues. Where do you stand on the following? What could go wrong?

- ☐ You share social networking with your peers.
- ☐ You share social networking with those you supervise (technicians, students).

☐ You share social networking with your PI.
☐ A student makes romantic advances towards you.
☐ Your PI asks you to babysit their children.
☐ The laboratory has an evening social in a bar once a week.
☐ Two postdocs in your laboratory start a relationship.
☐ Your department has a job opening which would be perfect for your partner.

* Where do you think might be the areas of potential relationship pitfalls in your current situation? What do you think you could do to avoid them?

Research records and data management

Effective management of your research project including organising, storing, and sharing research data is an essential component of good research practice. This includes the planning stages before the project begins, the day-to-day management, and the long-term storage and sharing of your data after the project finishes. Recently Research Councils UK (RCUK) and other research funding bodies have developed policies that put requirements in place for the researchers they fund to openly share their research data. Most universities will have a data management policy that will be available through their webpages or HR team that will help researchers to meet these requirements. Data security will be very important when dealing with human samples, personal data or patients.

There is a useful checklist for researchers on the UK Research Integrity Office (UKRIO) webpages that is taken from the UKRIO Code of Practice for Research.

Researchers should also be aware that there is a Concordat to Support Research Integrity to which UK Universities have signed up. "The concordat sets out five commitments that will provide assurances to government, the wider public and the international community that research in the UK continues to be underpinned by the highest standards of rigour and integrity."

Plagiarism and copyright

Plagiarism is a form of academic misconduct and involves using someone else's work or ideas without giving them the credit (and therefore the reader assuming the work is your own). It is also termed "literary theft" by some.

Scientific research invariably builds on the work of others. There are rules and laws that govern the use of other people's material in your own work. Having written a thesis and probably other research outputs, you will be aware of the conventions for citing and acknowledging other peoples work, and you will know that you shouldn't copy other people's work or claim credit for other people's ideas (either deliberately or inadvertently by not citing the appropriate reference), but where do you draw the line between what is acceptable use of other people's work and what is not acceptable?

Look at the list below taken from Swales and Feak (2012) and decide where you would draw the line between what is acceptable and what constitutes plagiarism:

☐ Copying a paragraph as it is from the source without any acknowledgement.

☐ Copying a paragraph making only small changes, such as replacing a few verbs or adjectives with synonyms.

☐ Cutting and pasting a paragraph by using sentences of the original but leaving one or two out, or by putting one or two sentences in a different order.

☐ Composing a paragraph by taking short standard phrases from a number of sources and putting them together with some words of your own.

☐ Paraphrasing a paragraph by rewriting with substantial changes in language and organisation, amount of detail, and examples.

☐ Quoting a paragraph by placing it in a block format with the source cited.

A note on self-plagiarism

One area that researchers are often unaware is that if you have written an article for a journal publication it is likely that you will have handed the copyright for that to the journal. Therefore, even though you have written the article and it is your work, if you then use that material elsewhere without properly accrediting the journal, you will be plagiarising.

Self-plagiarism — beware!

So, what exactly is copyright? Copyright in the UK is covered under law in the Copyright, Designs and Patents Act 1988. It provides legal protection to the creators of original works including literary and artistic works, sound recordings, film, and typographical arrangements. You must not copy a protected work without the permission of the copyright owner; if you do, you may be sued for damages.

Copyright on a piece of works exists automatically upon creation of the work. If you carry out a piece of work for an employer then usually the copyright belongs with them, but you should check your contract of employment for the details. If you are working with collaborators (industrial or otherwise) you need to check the agreements closely to see where your work on the project stands with respect to IP and copyright.

Conclusion

Professionalism and honesty should drive research and the environments where it is conducted. Postdocs as members of staff share this responsibility. The research arena is always shifting and bringing with it new ethical considerations. Today's science fiction may well be tomorrow's science fact and it is important to think through "what if or could be" scenarios to try and spot potential conflicts of interest before they arise. The current UK focus towards open access is a good case study: the science is not changing but the way we communicate and access it is. The ethics of open access and its consequences are evolving. What research publication will look like in 10 years is hard to predict but understanding your place in the shifting sands is very important.

What every postdoc needs to know about … research integrity and ethics

- ☑ Get familiar with your institution's rules on IP.
- ☑ Think about where you draw the boundaries in work relationships.
- ☑ Agree on a publication plan with your PI and other co-authors.

Resources

UK Research Integrity Office, available at www.ukrio.org/ which provides a check list for researchers — http://ukrio.org/wp-content/uploads/UKRIO-Recommended-Checklist-for-Researchers.pdf.

US Office of Research Integrity, available at http://ori.hhs.gov/education/products.

http://www.universitiesuk.ac.uk/policy-and-analysis/reports/Pages/research-concordat.aspx

Swales, J.M. and Feak, C.B. (2012) Academic Writing for Graduate Students. Essential Tasks and Skills, 3rd edition. The University of Michigan Press, Ann Arbor, MI, USA.

Chapter 14

Taking Responsibility for Your Career and Decision Making

Introduction

Your Principal Investigator (PI) is offered a chair at Harvard with a purpose built new laboratory, golden handshake and golf every Friday with the University Board. What are their first thoughts? Chances are that, although most PIs are great human beings, "What about my postdoc?" would not be among them. They might get to that question eventually after thinking about where they are going to live, the career prospects at that university, what it might mean for their family... They will, quite rightly, put themselves and their careers first. If postdocs want to be successful, then they need to learn to do the same.

Often when talking with postdocs it comes as a shock when we suggest to them that they might move onto the next career step (academic or otherwise) *before* the end of their contract. Their commitment to their project and their laboratory, even if the best thing they could do for themselves is move on, is admirable. But unless you have control of the job market (you do not), then the ideal job will not be waiting for you to step into when you are ready to apply for it.

It's your career

Your career is exactly that. Yours. You should be thinking about the next move/step up on day 1 of a new job. It is surprisingly common to start a first postdoc as "the next logical step" but having a clear onward goal can both be a great driver for success in the future and for your project. With this mindset everything you do during this postdoc should count towards your future goals. Focusing on goals should ensure time will be better spent and you will strive harder for measurable achievements (papers, grants, training, skills development, wider experiences). All those achievements will help secure the next position (academic or not). It will also help with the reference from this post. No one is suggesting you leave your post within 3 months of starting, but 6 months is regarded as the average time it would take to move from one role to another (think about advertising, applying, interviewing and a notice period — do you know your notice period?).

> A postdoc is not for life. Take as many opportunities to develop and learn wider skills than niche research knowledge. It is all good for a future career.
>
> James Suckling, Postdoc

∗ How long before you *must* start looking for the next role?

Some starting points to focus the mind. Work through the list below in order. Do not skip any questions with the "I'll come back later." It is our experience that successful postdocs plan out the next step early on, whether that step is academic or otherwise.

☐ When did your contract start (exact date)?
☐ When does your contract end (exact date)?[1]

---

[1] Ignore promises of potential extensions or "soft money" (extra money a PI might have)!

Take control of your career — no-one else will!

- ☐ What notice period do you have to serve?
- ☐ What avenues (outside academia) are you interested in?
- ☐ Where are these jobs advertised?
- ☐ Are there specific times of year when they are advertised?
- ☐ What is the success rate of people applying for these roles?
- ☐ How often are lectureships in your discipline advertised?
- ☐ Where (which websites) are lectureships in your field advertised?
- ☐ What fellowships are you eligible to apply for?
- ☐ What are the timelines for fellowships in your field?
- ☐ What is the success rate for fellowships in your field?
- ☐ Which organisations are employing postdocs like you?
- ☐ How much training and development can you undertake?
- ☐ What training and development opportunities are available to you through your current institution, and other organisations?
- ☐ How can you access these opportunities?
- ☐ Can you access help with applications/interviews/careers advice?

These may seem specific questions but being prepared, keeping an eye on job sites and using your network could help you spot that ideal next move. Postdocs who move on happily do so not because of luck but because they were ready to seize the opportunity when it came past. Also, do not fall into the trap of thinking no-one else is looking to move; they won't advertise the fact because they are in competition with you and may not want to talk with their PI about leaving until they have to/the deal is done. The first you often know that some-one is thinking of moving is when they come into the office in interview attire.

Decision making

Career decisions need to take into account both the work side of things and personal factors — such as where and who you want to live with, your values and your overall aims. Many postdocs find themselves in their first postdoc by almost flying auto-pilot through the education and higher education systems — one thing very much leading to another. If your postdoc is your first real job, then it is time to take control and start making some decisions. You may be target oriented with your eyes on a lec-tureship in 5 years' time. You may be more opportunistic, seizing challenges as they come along having weighed out the short term pros and cons. There is no right or wrong style but both come with their challenges. If your eye is on the big prize, you need to focus on the here and now to take the steps that will get you there. If your focus is more immediate you need to look ahead to ensure that you progress rather than randomly float between things. A balance of "strategic opportunism" is perhaps the ideal.

∗ How have you made decisions in the past? How did this work out for you?

Some people are paralysed at the thought of making a decision about their future. Others may seem somewhat cavalier. Thankfully, there is a system for both which should appeal to the rational, scientifically trained mind:

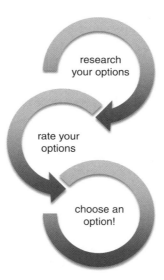

Bring your inherent research skills into play and find out as much as you can about your options using websites, your contacts, networking and visits, then an informed decision is much easier to make. Rate your options according to criteria you find most important such as salary, career progression, location, happiness (for more about rating, see the chapter on careers outside academia later). You should now have a rational analysis of your options. Admittedly at this stage you have to choose but this is not the end of the world. Is there a second option (plan B) that you could be working on alongside plan A? What steps do each have in common? Visualisation of yourself in the role 3 years forward can be helpful to some: what will you see, hear, touch, smell and feel (physically and mentally) when you get there. If you do not feel you can make a choice, then more research is in order. Luckily for you that is your job.

Self awareness of your skills, what you enjoy doing and what you are good at doing can also help with the decision making process. Often we work best, and are happiest, when working in a mode which makes us comfortable. If you are naturally a creative person to whom research ideas come thick and fast, chances are you would not be best suited to writing technical, precise equipment manuals. It's not that you cannot do it (after all our PhD has made us a Jack/Jill-of-all-trades) but it will be hard work. There are many "personality tests" out there varying from the social media (which Muppet character are you?) backed up with little research or evidence but a big "like count", to much more established tests backed up with research and normalised from a suitably large database. In general, the latter have some cost associated with them but may well shine a fresh light on your preferences. Some examples include Belbin Team Roles which gives you an insight into your preferred working style within a team, and Myers–Briggs type indicator (MBTI) personality inventory which aims to make the theory of psychological types described by C. G. Jung understandable and useful in people's lives (see Resources). Any test which incorporates the feedback of others is incredibly useful and may well show you talents which others see in you but you have perhaps dismissed.

If you are unsure about your options there are websites such as Pathmotion (see Resources) which can help you explore a variety of careers using your preferences in a variety of spheres as a starting point. Other methods of seeing "what else is out there" are discussed in the next chapter.

What if you get the decision wrong? This is not the end of the world. Our culture has moved very much away from the job-for-life setting of our parents and grandparents and people are much more mobile throughout their careers. Holding onto a clear idea of your skills and achievements will help you plot a course for the next step as well as building in the reflective learning from this small career blind alley. Chances are you will learn more from this situation than if you had landed the "right" job.

How many postdocs?

The question of "How many postdocs should I do?" is very similar to "How long is a piece of string?"... it depends. Postdocs vary in duration and different disciplines generate publishable results in different time frames. The best advice would be to look to those you deem successful in your field. Study those who are 3–5 years ahead of you and critique their trajectories. Older faculty members will have had very different experiences of their early careers — the academic scene is constantly shifting. One postdoc that generates good papers and puts you in a position to apply for a fellowship would perhaps be the most straightforward route but as we know, life is never that simple. It may be appropriate in some fields to gain industrial/public sector experience and then re-enter academia. The fact that there are few permanent academic positions compared with the number of postdocs is often "the elephant in the room."

When considering a further postdoc think long and hard about this question: what will this add to my CV? If the answer is more of the same then you may need to re-evaluate. If the postdoc adds a technique to your CV (and would therefore make you more employable outside academia or is essential to pursuing your own project) then it could be a good move. If your first project was multi-disciplinary it may be appropriate to use the second postdoc to deepen your knowledge of a new area. If you are only adding an employment line to your CV (just having a job) it may well be time to think of moving out of academia. It would be much better to explore other routes.

Some research institutions limit the time or number of contracts you can be a postdoc with them. The rationale is that it keeps both the research fresh and also encourages people to move onto all forms of careers. It might be an idea to impose something similar on your own career path.

* How will you avoid postdoc drift?

Will you be my mentor?[2]

Navigating any career path is difficult but there are those who have gone before. Seek people 3–5 years ahead of you in your chosen career path, consider asking for their help and advice. A first-hand perspective of different career trajectories may be highly beneficial to your planning. If you haven't chosen a route, ask several people!

The term mentor is often overused and confused but by engaging with people by asking intelligent, thoughtful questions, whilst being respectful of their views and time, you can build up a network of informal mentors who can advise you on different aspects of the career ladder. There are more formal mentoring schemes (seek out your institution or funder's schemes) which can be helpful in providing a framework and clear expectations for the mentoring conversation. But to paraphrase Sheryl Sandburg (see Resources) in her book "Lean In", a mentor is not a "mummy"! The relationship is a professional one where they will not provide all the answers for you but offer help and advice.

A coaching relationship is subtly different in that they will be there to support and guide you as a sounding board and will perhaps not offer direct advice but work towards you coming to your own conclusions. If you have informal coaching this may well look like informal mentoring but if you employ a career/life coach they may not have direct experience of your field.

Advice and feedback should be regarded as a gift. Accept it, thank the giver, evaluate its usefulness to yourself honestly and take on board what is helpful. At all times be respectful of the other person's time and energy. Be mindful that you too can provide this service perhaps to peers and students, if asked for.

∗ Who could you approach about being a mentor?

---

[2] We use the term mentor here to refer to someone other than someone who is your PI/supervisor/research mentor.

Drip, drip, drip, drop — the soft money trap

Consider the following scenario: A postdoc joins a laboratory and makes great strides. They rapidly get to be an expert in the techniques the lab uses and teach students effectively. They become somewhat indispensable to the PI. The support role eats away at their time and they just don't seem to be able to publish their work. The contract end approaches and the postdoc accepts an extension of funding for 6 months so they can write up their work. The funding comes from a small industrial project which gets promising results which can't be published for IP reasons. After 6 months another postdoc has left so there is 3 months' money for salary to finish up on their project. Those 3 months are consumed by working on a grant with the project data. The grant is submitted but a decision won't be made for another 6 months. The soft money has stopped. The salary stops and the University reclaims the swipe card to get into the laboratory.

Who shall we blame? The PI is an easy target — they should have been on top of the publications. The University — surely they could allow access to write up papers? These arguments could go round and round but the buck really stops with the postdoc. It is their career. First, they should have made the first postdoc count. Secondly, if papers weren't forthcoming readily, were they ever going to be? Thirdly, soft money to work on other projects whilst finishing up yours is working two jobs at once. With research jobs being so demanding, is this really feasible? Just ask anyone who has tried to finish writing up their PhD whilst starting a postdoc. The postdoc will have received warnings from their institution at various points near each contract end. Do not ever let this be an alarm bell or a surprise — you should have a plan of action (and be working on it) before any warning notification.

A little "cold shower"

We as authors hope this guide is upbeat and encouraging but we certainly do not want to sugar coat the reality! It is a job to get a job. That implies hard work, dedication and perseverance on top of what is already a pretty demanding role that often strays beyond the 9-to-5. So, it is very important to set aside time for career related activities even from your first day in your postdoc. Initially this may not be a huge amount of time, perhaps an hour or so a week, but getting settled into a routine with time where the focus is your future will ensure you know what is happening in the relevant job scene. Make sure you are signed up to helpful websites and set the filters so that you are getting the relevant information. When should this time ramp up? The clock should be ticking very loudly as you enter the final year of your postdoc and bearing in mind it can take 6 months to get a job, the primary focus of those last 6 months should be being able to eat and pay the rent, i.e. to get a job!

The other myth we would like to bust wide open is that postdocs in the UK are poorly paid. Yes, we know that "those city types" *can* earn millions but the average salary for someone in the finance sector in the UK is around £35k (source Monster, 2015). Current salary ranges for postdocs in the UK are around £31k–£40k usually depending on level of experience. The perception is that "industry" pays more and you have less freedom but the trouble with using blanket terms like "industry" is that it covers far too many options! Some may pay more; some may pay less. Private sector pay may also include benefits such as health insurance and nursery provision. The only way to combat this myth is to investigate the salaries for the roles you are looking at using job websites and salary calculators.

If you are considering moving out of academia then it is worth understanding that not every place will necessarily value your PhD — employers will be looking at the skills you have that are relevant to the role they are offering. A switch in careers may involve re-training or further study at the company's expense or you may need to build your experience level up. Both of these will require time (and therefore money) investing in you by the company and therefore a lower salary than you were expecting.

Conclusion

Armed with the understanding of your potential career routes, a grasp of your many skills and the readiness to undertake the job of getting a job, you are ready to embark on the next exciting career stage. The following chapters will help you do this, whatever your destination.

What every postdoc needs to know about ... taking responsibility for your career and decision making

- ☑ Your career is your responsibility.
- ☑ Make a plan ... one that will be reviewed and changed, no doubt, but you will achieve more with a plan than without one.
- ☑ Don't wait. Start planning from day one of your postdoc.

Resources

Belbin Team Roles, available at www.belbin.com

Meyers & Briggs Type Indicators, available at www.meyersbriggs.org

Career Inspiration from Pathmotion, available at www.pathmotion.com

Strategic optimism, available at https://hbr.org/1987/03/the-tactics-of-strategic-opportunism

The elephant in the lab, available at http://blog.wellcome.ac.uk/2013/01/28/postdoc-plan-b-the-elephant-in-the-lab/

Lean In: Women, Work, and the Will to Lead by Sheryl Sandburg Published by WH Allen (2015).

Monster, available at http://www.monster.co.uk/career-advice/article/uk-average-salary-graphs

Chapter 15

Careers Beyond Academia

Introduction

Become a gardener! This is my stock answer to the question I'm most asked by postdocs: "what else could I do?" They tend to look shocked and then come up with their own suggestions — which were there all along, they just hadn't been voiced.

Being a postdoc means that you have a lot going for you. You are highly educated (amongst the top 1%), literate, numerate, self-motivating, capable of team and independent work (in the main) and have undertaken an investigative project into an area that no-one else has studied which lasted at least 3 years. You are adept at seeking information, weighing up its usefulness and providing others with your conclusions. The fact is, the world needs people like you. We need teachers who understand investigative methods. We need business people who understand technology and mathematics. We need politicians who can weigh up the data they have been given. We need industrialists who appreciate research and development in all its many forms. In short, the world needs the skills you have spent years honing.

Often people feel like they are "giving up" research, and associated with this are feelings of loss and perhaps self betrayal or failure. It is common for people to have been moving toward a dream of being "a scientist", "an engineer" or "a mathematician" for many years. Being bright at school has led to getting into a good university from which a PhD followed naturally which then led into harnessing all that hard work by becoming a postdoc. Sometimes it is during this first postdoc that a researcher stops, takes a look around, and really questions where they are and where they are going. The postdoc stage is also when the realities of the academic job market start becoming apparent and peoples' natural priorities shift toward thoughts of houses, partners and families. Couple in the expectations of friends and families and being surrounded by academia, then it is not surprising that contemplating careers beyond the world of academia is an uncomfortable one. We may moan at the salaries, long working hours and the difficulties of obtaining a permanent position but we know the rules of engagement. It is our safe nest.

There's a wide world beyond the university walls.

But, for those who have made the leap, life goes on! We can still be "a scientist" by using the skills we have developed over at least 10 years of further study to tackle new problems and find solutions. Life outside academia is still intellectually challenging, socially important and flexible.

∗ How does the idea of moving away from academic research feel to you?

Searching

So, we are going to put our toe in the water and see what is out there. Where to start the search? If you are going to depart from the academic track, we would suggest initially a broad search for what is actually out there — even if you know which routes you are interested in. We may be experts in academic careers within, for example, biochemistry but the wealth of opportunities "out there" is vast.

How to begin a broad search? Our best advice would be to start somewhere new to open up your thinking. If you start to "google" there is a high chance that you will stick to sites you know. Set aside some time and space for this task (do not try to do this in the work environment especially if you are reluctantly looking at other options — you will get too distracted). A good method is to open up a traditional newspaper and look at the jobs pages (this could be done online but stick to the process). Don't just look at technical jobs or ones in the right location — look at ALL the jobs. This exercise is to open up your thinking. Ask yourself the following questions whilst doing this:

- ☐ Have I heard of this job/role before?
- ☐ Do I know what it entails? (there are often links to further particulars.)
- ☐ Do I match the skills they need? NB you don't need *all* the skills desired to be able to apply.
- ☐ How could I present the skills/experience I have to match those they want?
- ☐ Are there other things that my experience would add to the role?
- ☐ Is it a possibility?

If the answer to the last question having considered the others is "yes" then circle the job (if using paper!) or bookmark it. If the answer is "no" then cross it out (a door closed is useful!). If unsure then delve into the further particulars to find out more. Then move onto the next job. By the end of this process you will have a list of roles you could do, hopefully including some you would not have naturally thought of. This is a good starting point because it has got you thinking about roles, your skills and your preferences. There is also a need to learn the jargon of the job search much like that in a technical discipline. What exactly does "data analyst" or "project manager" mean in a specific context? If at any point your skin crawled at the thought of a certain role you have learnt something.

   ✳ Where and when will you start your broad search? Be specific and block time into your diary.

At this point it would be worth adding into this list other jobs and roles you would like to explore but didn't come from this initial search. You may already have ideas for these but, if you wish to expand your list, study your network (what do they do?) and look to those who have left your research group/department (what did they go on to do? could you talk to them about how they chose? what advice would they offer?).

Criteria	Questions
Salary	What is your salary now?
	How much of your outgoings are tied to your current role (commute, rental location)?
	What is the minimum salary you need (not want)?
	What are you basing this on?
	Have you thought about commuting costs?
	Employers may not pay a premium for someone with a PhD — especially if you have to be trained up for the role.
	A role may be a "stepping stone" into a new area, so a salary cut may be appropriate.
	Consider other benefits: health insurance, onsite nursery, company car/bike loans.
	What salary range would you be happy with?
Location	Can you move anywhere? In the world?
	What limits your location?
	Are you limited by visas or similar issues?
	Have you considered location effects on commuting, cost of living, quality of life?

(Continued)

Criteria	Questions
	Would this location suit you in 3 years time?
	Do you have access to childcare, schools, social activities here?
PhD essential	Does the role need a PhD?
	Will you resent it if people don't appreciate you having a PhD?
	How do you frame your PhD to match the job?
Team working	Would you be working in a team?
	Would you have management responsibility?
	What sort of teams would you like to work with?
Travel	Does the role offer opportunities to travel?
	Are you free to travel?
	Do you enjoy travel?
Intellectual challenge	Is it important to you to have a challenge?
Doing something in concert with your values and interests	What type of organisation would you like to work for?
	Are there industries you would prefer not to work with/for?
	What would you most like to work with? e.g. data or people
	Doing what? e.g. teaching, analysing, creating.
Part time/flexible working	Do you want to work part time?
	How much work do you want to "bring home"?
	Would you consider a job share?
	Have you factored in the salary pro-rata?

Narrowing

You now have a list (possibly quite a long one) of roles which you need to investigate further. In the scientific spirit we are going to weigh and measure these against various criteria. It is up to you to think about what criteria are important to you. When drawing up these criteria you may need to question these so that you do not limit your options unnecessarily. The following table outlines some possible criteria (by no means exhaustive and always worth having a "gut feeling" one too!) and the questions to pose to yourself. If you are having trouble with this, then ask someone you trust to act as a sounding board. Just as in recruiting it would not be fair to judge the roles without setting the criteria first but this judgement process can often inform us indirectly of our own personal preferences.

With a complete list of criteria we can now draw up a table where we can record facts and scores. The facts are important as too often we could tell ourselves something but have little idea as to whether that is the case. "Do you *think* that, or do you *know* that?" should be your mantra. Here research (from further particulars, web searches and your network) is essential. Once you have the facts then you can score for that criteria. Any scoring system that is useful to you could be used but the marks out of 10 system is as good as any. You should now have a table that looks something like:

Role	Salary	Score	Location	Score	—
R&D pharma			Stevenage	4/10	—
Patent attorney			London	7/10	—
Medical writer			Cambridge	7/10	—

If, after this, a job is coming out top which you are really not attracted to, think about why is that and what have you missed on your criteria table. You will find there are many, many roles you *could* do. This exercise is to help you find the ones you would *like* to do.

Translating your skills for the wider world

Not everyone has a PhD. Not everyone has worked in a research setting. These may seem obvious but we often are blind to the assumptions we make as to how others will view our achievements and skills. Those in your field will understand what those two first author papers in a leading journal represent. Unpacking the achievements and skills involved in those papers may include some or all of the following:

☐ project design,
☐ project management,

- ☐ attention to detail,
- ☐ negotiation,
- ☐ team work,
- ☐ people management,
- ☐ creativity,
- ☐ resilience,
- ☐ written communication skills,
- ☐ communicating technical arguments,
- ☐ ability to act on feedback,
- ☐ technical skills,
- ☐ data analysis,
- ☐ data display,
- ☐ insight,
- ☐ independent working,
- ☐ quality assurance.

The above is now looking much more like a person specification from a job advertisement. You will need to tap into your experience and skills and also help the employer looking at your application see where your experience will fit with the advertised role.

* Using the table below list your experience against these common job description criteria. You are providing evidence — make it as specific (and upbeat) as possible. Numbers, good feedback and achievements all add weight to this evidence.

Good communication skills
Management experience
Customer service
Negotiation
Training
Teamwork
Commercial/business awareness

Use your network

Job hunting and exploration is hard work. The often heard expression "It is a job to get a job" is very true. However, chances are that you know (or know someone who knows) a person who can help you with information and perspective on different career routes you are exploring. Universities and research institutes are very network driven and your existing network is probably larger than you think. You will have connections from your undergraduate studies, doctoral endeavours and from your postdoc. Building a network that can inform and help you make the correct next step for your career should be a priority as soon as you start your postdoc. If you apply the research skills you already have in abundance to "mining" your network you will put yourself in the best position.

Face-to-face networking is important but increasingly the initial "work" part of networking is done on the internet. There are many networking sites which for the purposes of job hunting could be divided into three categories (we realise this list is not complete):

☑ social — Facebook, Instagram, Pinterest, Twitter.
☑ research based — ResearchGate, Mendeley, Google Scholar.
☑ professional — LinkedIn, Twitter.

If you are considering a move away from academia then creating a LinkedIn profile would seem a sensible move. Firstly, it allows you to pull all your contacts in one place and from there taps into "who does your network know?" Before adding connections make sure your profile is up to date, reflects yourself in the best light and that you have a professional (not you on a beach) photo! Your "Summary" should give away more about you than a simple list of your CV (these facts are after all below the summary box) and includes keywords related to your job search. One simple way to improve your profile is to edit the "Professional

Headline" which follows you around the site under your name. If this simply holds a job title "Research Associate" you are missing a trick. Change it to something that reflects your skills and career direction, e.g. "quantum physicist and science communicator." Some simple ways of exploring options outside academia using LinkedIn are:

☑ Follow companies you are interested in and look at their job pages.
☑ Type a company name from the particular industry you are looking at into the search box. This may produce network links with people who work there.
☑ Type a role title into the search box. This will produce network links with people who have had or hold this title. It will also suggest groups you might consider joining.
☑ Use the tag facility and post relevant, interesting items to the right audience.

Networking will inevitably involve asking someone for some information. These requests should be polite and possibly more formal than a usual email. Clearly outlining what help you need and what you are trying to do will make it very straightforward for the person to respond. Never send an email asking for a job — these are unlikely to get a positive response but in general people are happy to help. Similarly, be prepared to help others when you are asked to help your own network.

"what goes around, comes around."

It would be a good idea to keep a note of what you ask for, to whom and at what point. You do not want to become a burden to those who have helped you and you want to ensure you have followed up leads. Another important piece of advice is to say thank you for everything, always. If a piece of information has not helped still say thank you, the person at the other end knows their message got there and it keeps the connection alive. If a nugget of job-seeking gold helps you land the next position do let the person who helped you know (and a brief handwritten thank you would be appropriate here).

Sample connect request

"Dear Jo,

I am exploring career options after my postdoc in organic chemistry. I am a talented communicator with several papers and outreach publications. I am considering a scientific publishing route. I would like to connect with John Smith at BigJournal as he has already made this transition. Could you introduce us on LinkedIn please?

Yours, Alex"

Sample request email

"Dear Jo,

I am exploring career options after my postdoc in organic chemistry. I am a talented communicator with several papers and outreach publications. I am considering a scientific publishing route. Given your experience as a journal editor I wondered if you could put me in contact with anyone who has made the transition from academia to publishing.

Yours, Alex"

Conclusion

There is a fabulous array of careers for postdocs willing to move away from academic research. But it can be difficult to "leave it all behind." Investigating your options, preparing Plans A, B (and C?) can ensure that any choice you make is grounded and informed. The act of working through job descriptions and seeing your skills in a different light can be most encouraging!

What every postdoc needs to know about ... careers beyond academia

☑ There are lots of possibilities for people with your skill set — don't let that put you off.
☑ Develop a strategy for investigating options.
☑ Try not to let the expectations of others hijack your choices.

Resources

Nature on the use of social networks by academics, available at http://www.nature.com/news/online-collaboration-scientists-and-the-social-network-1.15711.

http://jobsontoast.com.

http://www.jobs.ac.uk/careers-advice/studentships/1926/phds-applying-for-jobs-outside-academia.

https://www.findaphd.com/advice/doing/phd-non-academic-careers.aspx.

Chapter 16

Fellowships

Introduction

If you are a postdoc aiming to move on to an academic position you may choose to go via the fellowship route, i.e. move on from being a postdoc on someone else's grant to gaining your own funding to pursue your own research. It is not a guaranteed route to an academic position and by no means the only route to an academic post, but is a channel that has received attention and funding in the UK over the past few years. The League of European Universities (LERU) highlights fellowships on their career maps for several European countries.

So ... What is a fellowship? Generally speaking, a personal award, won competitively, which will allow you to pursue your own research direction within a host institution. In the sciences, these often cover salary and a budget towards consumables (the host institution may be expected to provide infrastructure and equipment as well as laboratory space). Fellowships are awarded by universities, charities, research councils and learned societies often on an annual basis. They are normally very competitive with success rates for some less than 10% and the funders are expecting world class research outputs in return (papers, grants, impact and professional prestige) i.e. funders want a return on their investment!

Why would you want one?

If you have a research idea you wish to pursue, a fellowship will enable you to concentrate on this idea without having to work on someone else's project. A fellowship will let you develop the skills associated with being a Principal Investigator (PI) (securing further funding, budget control, student supervision and management). Fellowships are often high profile and certainly prestigious. The best way of finding out what being a fellow is all about is to ask one. Current fellows are invaluable sources of information; from talking to you about their application (and perhaps giving you a copy), their experience of their interview and how they prepared for it, how they are conducting their fellowship and the benefits of running your own project.

∗ List the people with personal fellowships working at your institution.

A fellowship is a significant step towards an academic position but it is not the whole story. For example, at the end of the fellowship a fellow will need evidence of some if not all of the following: papers, patents, research outputs, conference presentations, invited talks, recognition and awards, independence, managing projects and people, managing finances, raising your professional profile and applying for and securing further funding. So, it is important to think carefully about what you are aiming to achieve from a fellowship. It is **significantly** different from being a postdoc on someone else's grant.

The award of a fellowship is testament to a peer review process where you have proved that you have the potential to be a research leader, you have the track record or potential to be research independent, you have demonstrated research excellence, and you have creative and exciting ideas in your field. All of the above is a fantastic launch pad for applying for academic posts but the focus is on you. Probably the most important thing to remember is that fellowships are a personal award. You need to demonstrate that you are moving forwards to an independent career, which means that you are not reliant on your former PhD supervisor or the Principal Investigator from a postdoc contract on which you were employed.

Demonstrating research independence is key to gaining a fellowship.

Fellows have a proven track record of:

☑ Research independence.
☑ Original research.
☑ Raising money.
☑ Supervising research students.

Research Councils UK (RCUK) is particularly committed to supporting fellows and state the purpose of a fellowship is to:

- attract excellent researchers into excellent UK research environments,
- develop research leaders for the future UK national capability,
- drive forward innovative areas of research.

(Continued)

(Continued)

The commitment from them as a funder is to:

- Award fellowships to outstanding individuals undertaking excellent research projects in excellent research and training environments.
- Provide, through the fellowship award, funding for a high quality research project and an ambitious programme of research training, personal development and leadership activities.
- Value fellows as important members of the Research Councils' wider research community.

RCUK 2015

Seeking fellowships

There are many different types of fellowship, with different schemes aimed at different career stages with each funder having their own quirks, systems and processes. So, where do you start hunting? Use your research and investigation skills which may include:

- ☑ First look within your department or institution to identify the fellows and where they received their funding from.
- ☑ Seek advice from colleagues.
- ☑ If you have a mentor — chat with her/him.
- ☑ Talk with the team within your institution that assists with funding applications.
- ☑ Investigate the research councils, charities and individual institutions' websites.
- ☑ If your institution has a subscription to Research Professional or another funding database then set up a search for funding in your discipline.
- ☑ Investigate professional bodies associated with your discipline.
- ☑ Look at wider European funding if you are from the EU or your home country may have fellowships.

Before starting your quest to apply for a fellowship, you need to find the right one for you, as well as the right one for your proposed department and institute, i.e. you need to do some background work because every fellowship is different. Finding out the answers to the following questions for all the fellowships you come across will help you to focus your research further on the most appropriate options for you. Use the checklist below to explore

☐ How many years (maximum/minimum) postdoc experience should I have?
☐ Do I need to move institutions?
☐ Does the application process include an interview?
☐ When are the entry dates?
☐ What is the gap in time from application to taking up post?
☐ How quickly are the decisions made?
☐ What is the duration of the fellowship funding?
☐ How much funding is available?
☐ What will it cost my host institution?
☐ Do I need to have a sponsor/mentor?
☐ Do I need external collaborators?
☐ What are the expectations of the fellowship e.g. measures of impact.
☐ Is there a possibility of continuation of funding after the initial award?
☐ Am I required to undertake some public engagement activities?
☐ Could I take this fellowship with me if I moved institution?

Maximising your success

Follow the rules

There is no such thing as guaranteed success but there are things you can do which increase your likelihood of being shortlisted. The shortlisting procedure will be about fit: to the criteria, person specification and research focus. Ensure you have chosen a fellowship scheme that is a good match for you and your project. The following pointers may sound obvious but we have seen many applications which break the rules — these will just end up on the "no" pile.

Make sure that your proposed research fits within the remit of the funder and also the specific programme to which you are applying. If your project fits, do you fit the eligibility criteria? Make sure, for example, you read the details of exactly when the years post-PhD are calculated from, any nationality requirements, and if the fellowship is aimed at a specific group (e.g. returners from maternity/paternity/parental leave). If you are not sure, talk with the programme/scheme/portfolio manager at the funding body; these conversations are always worth having because funders are keen to get good quality, eligible applications from which to choose.

Plan the application process for your chosen fellowship well … because it takes ages! Most people underestimate just how long it takes to write a fellowship application; getting approval from the institution, sign-off by the head of department and references by the sponsor and collaborators can all take a *very* long time. Find out about internal (to the proposed host institution) processes, i.e. are there any internal and/or department deadlines? Some fellowship funders will only allow a limited number of applications per institution. You don't want to spend months putting together an application only to discover that it will not be put forward because you missed the internal deadline or the quota of applications has already been reached. Plan each step of the process and factor in *realistic* timeframes (factor in iterations — you may need to write several drafts when you have received feedback from your sponsor, collaborators and head of department). This will include contacting any external contributors early, particularly if you need them to provide letters of support.

Refer to the guidance documents constantly, and make sure you are using the most up-to-date version. Do this to check you are following the rules and to ensure that you have included all the information they have asked for (also that you are not sending them information they have specifically said they do *not* want). Ensure that you know what all the deadlines are, acknowledging that the final "submit" button might be an institutional one so your deadline might not be the funder's deadline.

Assessing your application: The 3Ps

Fellowships differ from other sources of research funding and this is reflected in how they are assessed. Do check the assessment criteria but in general terms these criteria are the 3Ps: Person, Project and Place. The case you need to make must address these three things. They won't necessarily be assessed equally, but they will all be considered.

Person

Fellowships are personal awards and funders are looking to appoint future research leaders. You will need to demonstrate your research independence and make a strong case that this is not just more of what your current PI is doing, followed by a strong statement as to how this fellowship will advance your career as an independent researcher (see later). Why should they invest in you? Possible answers are:

☑ Your potential as a high calibre research leader.
☑ Your expertise in the field.
☑ Your track record.
☑ Your vision for the future of this research.
☑ Your potential to become a field leader.
☑ Your Past/current/future collaborations with industry.

Project

A fellowship is an investment by a funder to bring a research idea to fruition. They have many calls on their money. Your job is to convince them this is a more important/exciting project than anyone else's. Ask yourself this about your ideas:

- ☑ What is the context of this project?
- ☑ Are the research questions/hypotheses/objectives interesting and clear?
- ☑ Are the deliverables and outcomes achievable?
- ☑ Do you have any preliminary data or proof of concept?
- ☑ Why does this work need to be done now?
- ☑ Who will benefit from this research being undertaken?
- ☑ Is this work important and does it have value? — is the problem important in addressing any of the big questions in your academic field now?
- ☑ Is the project original, novel and exciting?
- ☑ Is it ambitious but feasible in the time and funding you have available?
- ☑ What will funder/stakeholders/the field/society lose if this research does not go ahead?

Place

You will need to justify your choice of research organisation — particularly if you are staying in the same place.

- ☑ What is the standing of the research organisation?
- ☑ What access to training will you have? Is there dedicated training for fellows?
- ☑ Why have you chosen this research group/department?
- ☑ What equipment do they have?
- ☑ What links do they have for making your research impactful?
- ☑ Is there the opportunity for you to develop your own expertise, or is there already a large, well-established group of which you will be part?

Your application is a written document and you are not there with it to explain to the reader any sections they do not quite "get".

Therefore, writing in a clear, logical and coherent manner is vital. Here are some points to consider:

- If you are including work packages make sure they relate directly to the overall project aims.
- Avoid acronyms and technical jargon. If you need to use technical jargon, make sure you explain it.
- Write a clear lay summary.
- The project title should be straightforward — you may have to live with it for several years.
- Check your spelling and grammar. Reviewers get extremely annoyed if a document is littered with spelling mistakes and grammatical errors. If a document is too badly put together, the reviewer will then wonder whether the poor quality and careless writing is reflected in the quality of the research work.
- Stick to the format of the applications e.g. font, margins, page and character count, even if this restricts what you can write.
- Make sure you understand and address the funders specific questions (e.g. "pathways to impact").

Fellowships are a personal award, not a grant and the assessment is of you as a researcher, not the group you are in, your PhD supervisor or your current PI. We have all been taught to write in the third person e.g. *the author notes that this is rather clumsy and stuffy,* but a number of sections on a fellowship form are likely to ask questions such as "What are the key questions **your** research will answer?", "Why are **you** the best candidate to undertake this research". For these sections, referring to yourself in the third person reads rather awkwardly and using "I", "My research", "the research questions I will be addressing" reads much better. It is also possible that referring to yourself in the third person may suggest that someone else wrote it. Similarly, if you overuse the words "we", "our" and "us", the reviewer may question what is your unique contribution and idea rather than that of a bigger group. Therefore, our advice is to use "I", "my", "mine".

The anatomy of an application

With competition high for most fellowship schemes, it is important that all parts of your application are strong. There is no room for a weak section. Here are some tips and common features on fellowship application forms with examples taken from the Junior Research Fellowship Application form, Imperial College London.

Project title

Is it understandable? Would a member of the public know what you are doing? Remember if the turn-around time for a fellowship application is a year and it's a 3-year fellowship, you'll need to "live with" the title for 4 years, so be careful of the WiTiAcroNyM that seems clever or funny at the time but turns out to be difficult to spell and annoying in the longer term! If you want to see examples of titles, go to funders' websites, weekly column in the Times Higher and examples from the fellows in your department.

Head of Department approval

Many fellowships include consumables but not overheads (such as heating, lighting, I.T., estates maintenance) so the department may be subsidising the project and, for research which includes expensive equipment, it almost certainly will. Talk to the head of your proposed host department and present a convincing case why they should support you. Make sure what you are doing both fits in and is complementary to what the department already does. If the Head of Department does not support your application, then you will need to take it somewhere else. A Head of Department is not obliged to support a fellowship application, even if it is good.

Letters of support

Letters of support are usually given by past or potential collaborators. Letters of support could be viewed as references and our experience has been that some people choose someone senior who has little idea about them. Therefore, ensure that the people you have asked to write a letter of support:

- Know you.
- Know your research.
- Are positive about your research.
- Will write you a *positive* letter of support.
- If offering to host you, that it is a genuine offer rather than inviting you to be a senior postdoc in their lab.

Confidential letter of support

This is different from the letter from your sponsor and the letter from any potential collaborator. If you are asked to draft the confidential letter of support yourself (it does happen) you may want to rethink who you ask for a confidential letter of support. Good people to ask are your current PI (assuming they are not your proposed sponsor), your PhD supervisor, a collaborator or a senior postdoc in your lab. It is key that you ask someone who you know will write a good letter, and who knows both you and the work you have done so far.

Funding request/budget

This section usually covers your salary costs, consumables, travel and miscellaneous expenditure. Read the background information carefully. If you are already paid at a higher level than the salary range stated, the funder might not match this, so you need to seek additional funding from the host institution or be prepared to take a salary cut. If you are a postdoc, the "source of funding" is likely to be a research council, charity or another external funder. It is unlikely to be your institution. If asked to state your current salary, don't be tempted to give yourself a pay rise!

Read carefully what they are willing and not willing to pay for and what is the maximum amount you can request. If your research is expensive (e.g. animal work, laser beam time) and you have estimated that the money you need to do your fellowship is significantly higher than the amount they are willing to pay you will need to:

- Check with the funder and find out if the maximum they are stating really is the maximum (usually it is).
- Ask your proposed sponsor if they have any funds which you could access (this can happen but your sponsor may feel that they therefore should be on all your papers — see later section on choosing a sponsor).
- Identify future funding sources which, if you got the fellowship you would be able to apply for e.g. Young investigator awards. You will need to convince the funder that should you not get this extra funding the proposed research project is still viable.

Some fellowship applications request a lot of detail on the costs of your research, others may just divide the costs into broader sections such as consumables, travel and miscellaneous which could include open access charges and equipment. It is important to budget realistically so that the project is feasible with the resources requested. Funders will not be impressed by a research proposal that is cheap but has cut corners or has not considered the true costs associated with the research.

For travel expenses, remember that a fellowship is a great opportunity for you to launch your career and as such you should aim to attend (at the very least) the key conferences in your discipline. You should state what these conferences are, when they occur, and where they are normally held to budget for flights, conference registration and accommodation. Some fellowships ask for a justification of the funds which you have requested so that they can show value for money.

Lay summary

The lay summary is one of the most important but neglected sections on any fellowship application form. It is important because it is read by everyone regardless of their research expertise. It may also be used for publicity purposes (websites) and is the "high level" explanation of what your project is about. Many lay summaries, however, are written in a hurry near the deadline and are therefore not as readable as they should be. A quick check list of do's and don'ts in a lay summary:

☑ Do stick to the word limit — don't go over and don't go radically under. If it says 300 words maximum, aim for that.
☑ Do write a summary which an intelligent, non-specialist adult could understand.
☑ Do write in plain English.
☑ Do ensure that the summary fully covers what you will be doing.
☑ Do ask for feedback from a variety of people.
☒ **Don't** use jargon or acronyms.
☒ **Don't** make it boring.
☒ **Don't** leave it until the end.

Research question and aims

You need to identify a question or questions that your research will aim to answer. If this section says, "What are the key questions that you wish to answer" you should answer using the first person e.g. "I plan to" …. Ensure the questions are interesting and exciting, can be answered, and are achievable in the timeframe of your fellowship. Don't pose questions which will need an army of people to work on. You may also want to include details of the hypothesis you will be testing, your research philosophy and your overall objectives for the project.

Background

This section usually includes the context of the research, and may ask why you are the best person to do the research. Again, use the first person. This is your opportunity to give background information about where your research fits in with previous work in this area and in your discipline, why it is important to do this research, and why your previous experience makes you (and only you) the person to carry out this research. It is more about you than the standard literature review!

Research plan

It is unlikely that the assessors want a detailed, week by week plan, but they will want to see milestones and deliverables, perhaps presentations at meetings, long-term experiment runs, clear deadlines for sample collection and analysis. A Gantt chart is a visually clear and effective way to present this information which assessment panel members will value. If the project includes visits to collaborators and other labs, these could be included.

Impact of the research

Measuring impact of research has become high on the agenda for funders and this includes fellowship funding — such as the new criteria and emphasis in the Research Excellence Framework (REF) (see Chapter 2 for information on the REF). Most funders will want to see what the potential impact of the proposed research is. Get help from your university support/bid development team to prepare this section, and remember to think widely in terms of social, economic, academic impact and beneficiaries. You are asked to consider *potential* impact so don't let your internal editor weigh you down with too much reality — this is where you can think big. Demanding that there is impact from research is controversial as some academics argue that this restricts "blue sky" research and many of our greatest research breakthroughs were "accidents" e.g. Penicillin. Some funders do not have an impact section e.g. Leverhulme because they want to support research without putting in the restriction that all research must have a measurable impact.

The award of a fellowship to further your career

It is acknowledged that the majority of fellowship holders move on to become highly successful researchers. Having a fellowship could be seen as the first steps to becoming an academic leader in your field. The funders are investing in you and they want to know what your career plans will be if you are awarded the fellowship. Use this section to really sell your view of your career and your ambitions. The funder is investing in you and DOES NOT want to hear the following (even if some of it is true).

- ☒ I want a permanent job.
- ☒ I enjoy what I do and just want to continue doing the same.
- ☒ I enjoy teaching.
- ☒ I want to stay in the same lab/group.
- ☒ I don't want to move.
- ☒ I did my degree, masters, PhD, 3 years of a postdoc at this institute and want to stay.
- ☒ I want a pay rise.

They are likely to be impressed if you include the following:

- ☑ The award of this fellowship will allow me to focus on these significant challenges in partnership with international collaborators.
- ☑ My aim is to run my own research group which will tackle interesting and significant challenges.
- ☑ In 5 years' time I aim to be a leading academic in this field.
- ☑ At the end of this fellowship I will have developed the understanding of this topic in an interesting way.

∗ At this point in this chapter — think about what a fellowship would do for your career.

Your choice of sponsor

Many fellowships will require you to secure a "sponsor" or "mentor" for your research. It is important to think very carefully about your choice of sponsor. Your sponsor **is not** your supervisor, nor is he/she the Principal Investigator of your project — you are. However, they are likely to be "hosting" you in their lab and if the fellowship you have been awarded does not include full economic costs and/or overheads, they may also be subsidising your project in terms of lab space, equipment and consumables. The relationship with your sponsor can be tricky. On the one hand they will want to support you and encourage you in your fellowship — you are, after all, a potential future colleague, but in a system of tighter spending and limited resources, they will, understandably, want to know what they will gain from sponsoring you.

So, how to choose your sponsor? Fellowships are about research independence. If you decide to choose a sponsor who was previously your PhD supervisor or PI, you are likely to find it difficult to prove that you are research independent. Why? Because papers written during your fellowship may have your sponsor's name on them and therefore anyone externally assessing your CV and publications list may assume that you will, in effect, continue to be a postdoc in the lab of your sponsor. This will not help your career. Some fellowships insist that you move institution to avoid this situation, but if you are staying in the same department, the same group, and the same lab, you will have to make an extremely strong case for why you are doing this. It could, potentially, damage your application because the assessors are not convinced that by the end of the fellowship you will have proved that you are research independent.

So, who should your sponsor be? From discussions with current and past fellowship holders, although it is tempting to choose someone very senior e.g. a Head of Department, a senior Professor, an academic who runs a very large group and has a wide portfolio of external activities, in reality you are unlikely to have very much of their time. Perhaps a better question to ask yourself is "What do I want from my sponsor?" Being able to answer this question will then help you to identify the best person to be your sponsor. For example: are they experts in a particular technique which you would like to learn? Do they have equipment you need to use?

Is their work complementary to what you are aiming to do and therefore both will benefit?

When approaching your potential sponsor be very clear as to what you want from them. Some schemes will only allow a sponsor to host one fellow and therefore as well as you selecting them, they may have been approached by a number of potential applicants and will be deciding whether to select you or someone else.

And finally.... Make sure you select someone who you know will write you a good reference. We know this sounds obvious but we have seen references from people who clearly didn't know the candidate at all. Talk to them, discuss your proposal, your career ambitions and how your work will benefit and complement their work.

Conclusion

And finally... a check list of questions:

- ☐ Is your project realistic, well-thought through and well-conceived?
- ☐ Is the amount of work you have allocated both feasible in terms of time and resources?
- ☐ Is your project well written, with no spelling mistakes, grammatical errors and with all sections complete?
- ☐ Is it understandable to an intelligent non-expert?
- ☐ Is the pitch for independence clear and you are not doing more of what your current PI is doing?
- ☐ Is your research vision clear and concise?
- ☐ Do you have a sufficient track record i.e. papers from your PhD or the years you've been a postdoc?
- ☐ Do you have preliminary data or proof of concept?

Gaining a fellowship will be a tremendous springboard for you to move forward to an academic career. They are highly competitive but also rewarding and a great opportunity for you to be research independent, to start to grow a research group and to build your reputation as a serious and successful researcher.

What every postdoc needs to know about ... fellowships

- ☑ Can be the start of your independent research career.
- ☑ Get organised early and plan the application process well.
- ☑ Ask for feedback and help at each stage.

Resources

League of European Universities (LERU) career maps, available at http://www.leru.org/files/general/UK-England.pdf

Research Professional site for a wealth of information, available at https://www.researchprofessional.com

Research Councils UK (RCUK), available at www.rcuk.ac.uk

The Wellcome Trust, available at http://www.wellcome.ac.uk

Chapter 17

The "Lectureship Leap" (Lectureships: What are They and How To Apply)

Introduction

Being a lecturer is, ironically, not all about lecturing! So, what is it about, and what do you need to do to become a lecturer? We will examine these topics in this chapter. Many will say that the route to a lectureship is to get a fellowship first (see Chapter 16). Although getting a fellowship can certainly help in your aim to get a lectureship in some institutions, it is not a guaranteed move. The benefits of getting a fellowship are that you have already proved that you are an independent researcher (or have the potential to be), have written and/or contributed to research papers, and that you are generating interesting ideas for research projects. But what else does every postdoc need to know?

The harsh reality

From our work with postdocs we know that the vast majority of postdocs want to become academics, but we also know the odds are not good. Research has shown that <10% of postdocs in the UK will eventually get an academic job in the UK and if you work at a research-intensive university the chances of staying at the same university and successfully applying for a lectureship are extremely low.

Whilst becoming a lecturer appears to be the next obvious step on the academic career path, frequently postdocs either don't really know what working as an academic entails or don't pause to ask themselves the question about **why** they want a lectureship. There is a danger of "postdoc drift" turning into "lectureship drift" but, with the competition for jobs high, this is more of a "lectureship leap"!

* So, what should you do? Firstly, ask yourself the following questions:

☐ Why do I want a lectureship?
☐ What are the pros and cons of getting a lectureship?
☐ Do I really know what a lectureship is and what is involved in the role?
☐ Have I talked to someone who is a few years further (not too far — lecturing has changed) on in their career, who has a lectureship and who can give me honest feedback about the challenges of being a lecturer? What have I learned from this conversation?
☐ How much teaching have I done? Do I like teaching?
☐ What experience of writing grants have I had?
☐ What type of institution would I like to work in? — Teaching-led, research-intensive?
☐ How good is my time management?

When you've answered the questions and maybe talked through your answers with a colleague or a mentor, if you still want to be a lecturer then the next step is to start thinking about what skills and experience you need to develop and have evidence of so that you can secure a lectureship. Then you can start to do some research into lectureships; what is currently being advertised and where are these jobs?

Skills and experience

The work of a lecturer can usually be roughly divided into three main parts: teaching, research and administration, and therefore selection criteria for lectureships will be using these three main areas (see later in the chapter). You need to be realistic about your skills and past experience and review what you need to do to fill out the form effectively. Later in this chapter we look at specific sections on a lectureship form but first it is worth making a list of everything you could evidence of your experience in teaching, research and administration.

∗   Your evidence for teaching.
∗   Your evidence for research.
∗   Your evidence for administration.
∗   Now ask yourself — where are the gaps? What do I need to do more of?

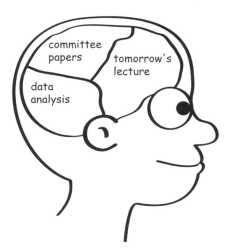

Being a lecturer is splitting yourself in 3: research, administration and teaching.

Another way to help identify the evidence you will need is to find examples of lectureship application forms from the type of university you would like to work in and evaluate your current skills and experience in relation to what they are looking for.

We are frequently asked the following questions…, "How many papers do I need to get a lectureship? How many grants do I need to have? How much teaching do I need to do?" Every discipline is different, therefore providing guidelines for these will be meaningless. However, what you can do is research the "norms" of your discipline. Conference proceedings, for example, have far greater standing and significance in computing subjects than they do in the biosciences. Talk to people in your department, ask to see their CVs (they may be on their personal web pages), find out the "average" number of papers it would be expected that a good academic produces every year. Similarly, you can research the funding income and teaching experience of those who have recently made the transition from being a postdoc to a lecturer in your discipline, so that you can understand whether your level of experience is above or below average. Please note, more is not always better! For example, some may view a smaller amount of varied teaching experience more favourably than vast amounts of laboratory demonstrating experience.

For research it is important for you to demonstrate that you are an independent researcher, i.e. that your work has come from your original ideas and that you have been the lead researcher on the project. If you have thought about applying for a fellowship (see Chapter 16) you face the same challenges, i.e. if you have stayed in the same department for all your studentships (undergraduate degree, masters level degree and doctorate) and for your postdoc, it will be extremely difficult for you to demonstrate research independence from the supervisor/PI you have been working with. Many postdocs make the mistake of identifying themselves too closely with the group leader by highlighting in applications that they are e.g. "a member of Professor Smith's research team." This simply emphasises that you have worked for someone else, and does not help to establish your potential as an independent researcher and future research leader.

∗   What evidence do you have of research independence?

A further criterion for successful lectureship applications can be an assessment of national and international standing. How do you measure national and international standing?

☑ Papers in international journals?
☑ Talks at conferences?
☑ Invitations to speak at conferences?
☑ Peer-reviewed work?
☑ Submitted to the REF?

Other sections which you need to reflect on are:

* Collaborations — who are your current collaborators? Are they yours or part of the wider group/your Principal Investigators (PIs)?
* What funding have you applied for? Have you contributed to any grants which your PI is lead on? Have you applied for any internal funding?
* Widening participation activities and "public service" public engagement.
* Contributions to your department/school e.g. first aider, organiser of journal club, postdoc rep on Faculty research committee ...

Lectureship application forms and what you should include

Remember that universities are looking for exceptional candidates who will enhance the work of the institute. Some application forms are long and ask for a lot of information, others are shorter but the individual sections are more open ended. We have reviewed a number of lectureship application forms and selected the most common information for a lectureship to look at in detail.

Membership of professional bodies/learned societies

Are you a member of a professional body? If not, why not? Membership of a professional body shows your commitment to your discipline. Applying for membership may also mean that you have been assessed by your peers as having a particular academic standing.

Employment to include a brief description of responsibilities

Include only those appointments, which are relevant, i.e. other postdoc positions, industry roles, or "academic" work whilst studying for your PhD such as teaching and demonstrating. You do not need to include all vacation jobs but do include any relevant positions or those that demonstrate different skills sets e.g. project management, organisational skills, managing people, or show what you were doing if there would otherwise be a large gap in the timeline of your CV.

Details of past and current contribution to teaching including innovation and/or creativity in teaching to improve student learning

This is a broad definition of teaching and, even if you haven't done much "official" teaching or given a lecture, you are still likely to have made a contribution to teaching through day-to-day supervision of students, training team members on a piece of equipment or in a certain technique, or through mentoring or coaching others, for example. There are often opportunities to deliver workshops to research students through Researcher Development Programmes or Graduate Schools. If you are applying to a research-intensive university, many postdocs think that teaching is not important. The folklore of "teaching doesn't matter at research-intensive universities" is not true!

Some useful questions to ask yourself:

- ☑ What is my teaching philosophy?
- ☑ Which courses have I taught? Level, subject?
- ☑ What type of teaching was it? Seminars, tutorials, practicals, problem-solving classes, lectures, supervision, masterclasses…?

☑ What is the impact of my teaching?

☑ What evidence do I have of the quality of my teaching? e.g. student feedback.

☑ Have I gained experience of providing student feedback and assessment? What methods of assessment have I used?

☑ What creative or innovative teaching methods have I introduced?

☑ How do I ensure that all students' learning needs are met?

See Chapter 7 for more about teaching.

Research grants and contracts obtained over the last 5 years

If this section is blank, it would be highly unlikely that you would be shortlisted; but, if you have gained a fellowship, a travel grant, significantly contributed to a grant (as named researcher or Co-PI), this can be added here. It would not be expected that you will have been awarded significant amounts of money at this stage in your career but being awarded travel grants to attend a conference is good evidence that you know what you need to do to move in to an academic position.

Publications

☑ Refereed full papers.
☑ Refereed conference papers.
☑ Conference abstracts.
☑ Books and/or book chapters.
☑ Patents.
☑ Other.

This is a ranked list very commonly found on Science Technology Engineering Maths (STEM) focused application forms and therefore interesting to note when planning your writing schedule. It is refereed full papers which will count towards Research Excellence Framework (REF) in STEM (although monographs and books may be more prestigious in Law or Music) and will make you an attractive candidate. These papers need to have been written within the last 5 years and also include an explanation as to their impact, why the papers are important and what the key points are. If you have been submitted to the REF, you will need to state it here.

Referees

Your referees will be asked to provide a reference or recommendation on you and your work, and their opinions are an important part of the application. Many institutions will only allow you to use one referee from your current institution. If this is the case, then the referee will need to be your line manager i.e. your current PI. In selecting your referees, make sure you know they will write you a good reference. We know it sounds obvious, why would you pick someone who would write you a poor reference? But, we have seen many applications fail because the references are "lukewarm", perhaps written by someone whom you have not kept in touch with and so they are unable to write about your current work, or provided by someone who has asked you to write the reference yourself.

Research: current research, your major contributions to date. Outline your 5-year research plan

This section is a significant part of the application. Your task is to describe your current research, your future plans but to make sure that what you are aiming to do in your research is both complementary to what the department you are applying to does already and is also innovative and interesting. You need to have a very clear vision as to what you want to have achieved in 5 years' time. At this stage you should have a 5-year research plan which includes funding, growth of a research group, how many PhD students/postdocs you will need to carry out the research and where you will be applying for funding. This section presents an opportunity for you to illustrate your knowledge and understanding of research in your discipline and what your long-term aims are for that work.

Management, administrative and other relevant activities.

If you have organised a journal club, been a postdoc representative, worked on a committee, organised a research seminar series, been a member of an Athena SWAN self assessment team — these are all examples of administrative and other relevant activities. If you are just starting to look at lectureships and this section would be blank, ensure you volunteer to run a journal club or reading group (for example) so that you can add that activity to this section.

Personal development and developing others

This section should include any professional and personal development you have undertaken both in relation to transferable skills development and within your discipline. As part of your contract many institutions state the importance of continuous professional development, courses which are compulsory e.g. Health and Safety, training for undergraduate teaching and the benefits of mentoring. Even though you may not be formally supervising PhD students you may be providing mentoring and coaching.

Evidence of esteem, external visibility and professional activities

If you have been given an award, been invited to run a workshop, given a guest lecture, appointed on an external panel or board these are all activities which need to be described here. You could also include any peer review work you may have done, consultancy work or setting up of a spin out company.

Conclusion

Moving from a postdoc to a lectureship is a big leap. It is also very competitive and one of your biggest challenges is to provide the evidence that you have already done much of what is required of a lecturer i.e. teaching and independent research or that you have the potential to do so. If you want to become an academic, you need to start gathering the experience and evidence as soon as possible to make yourself a strong candidate.

What every postdoc needs to know about ... getting a lectureship

- ☑ There is no automatic step from a postdoc to a lectureship.
- ☑ Assess the skills and experience required for lectureships and take action during your postdoc to gain these.
- ☑ When you have seen a lectureship advertised in your field, do background research on the type of university it is e.g. research-intensive, teaching-led and assess whether you are a good fit.

Resources

Lectureship advice from jobs.ac.uk, available at http://www.jobs.ac.uk/careers-advice/working-in-higher-education/1057/how-to-become-a-lecturer

The National Careers Service has a good description and further links, available at https://nationalcareersservice.direct.gov.uk/advice/planning/jobprofiles/Pages/highereducationlecturer.aspx

A view on being a an early career lecturer, available at https://psimpsongeography.wordpress.com/2011/08/01/being-an-early-career-lecturer/

Chapter 18

How to Write a Winning Curriculum Vitae (CV)

Introduction

The information and advice in this chapter is designed to help you develop a CV which stands out from the crowd. Our recommendations are designed to make sure you have a CV which is fit for purpose, adapted to the particular job you are applying for, and all your skills and experience are easy to identify by a recruiter. Much of the information in this chapter is "best practice." Ultimately, it is *your* CV and when you submit it, you need to feel it truly reflects the skills and expertise you have and how you strongly match the job. You need to be proud of it and believe that you have put together the best CV you can for the particular job you are applying for. Please be assured that by following the guidelines in this chapter your CV will still be highly individual (some postdocs are concerned that their CV will look like everyone else's), but will be clearly laid out without basic mistakes and irrelevant information.

The purpose of a CV is to get you to the next stage of selection in a competitive process e.g. an interview for a job, the next stage of a funding bid, or for an application to join a professional body. CVs should be organic, highly flexible documents, which should be changed and adapted to every job you are applying for. A generic CV, which has not been tailored to the particulars of a job description, can be identified very easily and will likely be rejected. It is your job to present to the recruiter why you are the best candidate. Don't make the recruiter work for the information. For example, if you are applying for a teaching-only job, don't put all your teaching experience and skills in the middle of the document. Unless you have to fill out a CV from a template in an online application form for example, then don't use one. Templates force you to put your information into particular sections, which may not be the best way of illustrating the skills and experience you have.

Is the content relevant?

It is good practice to keep an up to date record of your activities, roles and achievements, including courses you have attended. You should also keep a record of examinations and qualifications with dates and a full career history with start and end dates for each role. We recommend having all this in one file or "master document" that is edited regularly.

Does all this need to be on your CV? No! Many CVs we see contain everything the person had ever done from school onwards. Everything has been added without any reflection on whether the information is relevant. "Full clean driving licence" is an example of this — unless the job you are applying for specifically asks for a driving licence, remove it and use the space for something relevant.

So, how do you choose what to put on your CV? Go back to your master file of everything you have ever done and view each piece of information as a Lego brick (or construction toy of your choice). The job description or funding call now acts as the instruction manual to create the perfect model CV. Within the job description highlight the key skills and experience that the recipient of your CV wants to see. These are the Lego bricks which need including. Often these are listed in order of importance, which then gives you a structure to your CV. The precise format will depend on the CVs destination.

Your skills and experience form the building blocks of your CV.

For each skill or experience on the job description, match up what you have to offer from your master document. Do not panic if you have nothing immediately — can you reframe some of your experience? For instance, supervising students could be management experience. Echo the words used in the description as you write your CV with the aim of making it very obvious you have these skills. Look at the experiences you have left out — are any of them potential value-added skills you could bring to the role? Only include them if it helps strengthen your case.

In general, you need to focus on the last 5 years and for anything older than that (excluding your qualifications) ask yourself if it is relevant to the job you are applying for and if it isn't then take it off. Given you are by this stage a research professional with at least two degrees you can remove your secondary school grades.

A CV should also reflect you and your achievements in a positive light. This might seem obvious but we have worked with CVs that highlight what we like to call "dis-achievements". These would include grants you have applied for and not won, coming third in a poster competition and papers that were rejected. Why list the mountains you have yet to climb? Positivity also needs to shine through in the language by using strong, active words in moderation: "led, investigated, discovered and created."

✳ Take a good look at your CV now — what could come across as negative?

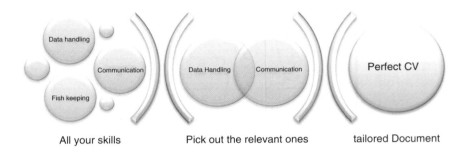

All your skills   Pick out the relevant ones   tailored Document

Is it tailored to the sector and job?

You need to make your CV look "local" i.e. that it fits in. Research and find examples of CVs used for the particular sector that you are applying to. CVs have cultural norms depending on where you are applying to and which country. If, for example you are applying to work at an academic institute in Singapore, you will need to include a photograph on the first page of your CV. In the UK we do not usually include photographs on CVs. If you are applying for a post in the USA your CV will be called a resume and may need to be shorter.

In terms of applying for jobs, you need to spend on average at least a day per application. Some recruiters require you to fill out an application form as well as a CV. Do not be tempted to send in a generic CV even though much of the information on your CV may be duplicated on the application form. Ask yourself "What additional, relevant information can I put on my CV that is not included on the application form?" You have much more opportunity for emphasis (what will you choose for them to read first?) on a CV compared to an application form.

Changing your CV for each job that you apply for is time-consuming and not easy. It may be tempting to put everything you can think of on your CV, because everything you have done is significant and important to you. You may be particularly proud of a prize you received when an undergraduate and this is put in pride of place on the first page of your CV. What you think is important may be completely unimportant to the recruiter. Ask yourself when adapting your CV for the next application "Why am I telling them this?" e.g. If you are applying for a fellowship and the fellowship details specifically state that "this fellowship is for research only and the funder will not support any teaching activities..." why would you include details of teaching activities on the front page of your CV for that application? Or if you were applying for a finance position, why would you put most emphasis on your research and papers? If you are unable to answer the question "Why am I telling them this?" then that particular section may need to be taken off your CV for that application. Warning! This can be painful, especially if you have invested time, energy, love and devotion to something that needs to be removed from your CV (we still mourn the loss of parts of our CVs). The first time you change your CV it will take a significant amount of time, but it becomes easier and quicker.

The only use for an "instant" CV is when you have to react very quickly which is usually in response to an unexpected opportunity (job hunting is not in this category!). For instance, someone asks if you would like to be on a panel to fill in for a missing speaker and ask for your CV to pass to the organisers. Having two or three versions of your CV "a click away" to answer this type of call is useful. Each version could be tailored though such as "academic me", "consultancy me" or "public engagement me".

Best practice for adapting your CV

The main message is that adapting your CV is largely about changing the layout and emphasis. You cannot change what you have done so far in your career, nor what your qualifications are or what your previous jobs have been. Keep in mind the 20 second rule — in a first pass, 20 seconds is probably the amount of time that your recruiter will take to look at your CV. "Hook" them by giving them the relevant information on page 1. Make it stand out and give the right message.

∗   Get someone else to look at your CV for 20 seconds — what do they pick up?

If you are thinking of moving out of academia, your CV needs to emphasise different things to an academic CV. What is valued within academia e.g. qualifications, papers, national and international reputation may not be valued to the same degree in other sectors. A patent attorney may not be interested in the fact that you've written papers with a high impact factor and which papers have been highly cited, but they will be interested in your ability to write clear, concise reports, to a deadline and at an appropriate level. So, again, it is about changing the emphasis and "re-packaging" your experience in a way that will clearly communicate your suitability and fit for the job you are applying for. Do not assume that everyone reading your CV will understand the wealth of skills represented by the simple "5 first author research papers." You need to clearly state you have project and time management skills in addition to excellent written communication and editing skills. Not everyone understands how wonderfully talented the postdoc community is! In general, non-academic CVs are shorter than academic CVs but again, do some research to check the "norms".

Follow their rules!

If the CV says "please submit a 2-page CV, Arial size 12" do just that even if all the previous versions of your CV are long and crafted in your favourite font. They will have chosen the format so it is easy for them (the recruiter) to read. If your CV is currently longer than 2 pages, do not change the margins in order to "cram in" all the information you currently have on your CV. If you take the margins out or reduce the font size to 8 or 9 it will be difficult to read. It will fail the 20 second rule as it is unlikely anyone will persevere if it is too difficult to read. It will go on the "no" pile and they will move on to the next person's CV. Once your CV is on the "no" pile it is likely to remain there. If there is no guidance, your mantra should be "make it easy for the recruiter to read."

Currently, we are in a selectors market i.e. employers are able to "select" from a number of very good candidates rather than recruit in "desperation" to fill a post. For many posts there will be a large number of applications, and the recruiter will be unable to spend more than a few minutes initially screening applications. Part of that initial screening will be checking that you have supplied all the requested sections in the correct format.

Your CV file/layout

Your CV needs to get to the recruiter in one piece, tailored to them and ready to be printed and copied. A few simple rules are:

☑ Save your CV in pdf format, this will avoid the layout being changed if someone is viewing it on a different software system to the one you wrote it on e.g. Mac to PC and vice versa.

☑ If you have had lots of feedback, double check that the CV you submit does not have any comments or tracked changes on it.

☑ Ensure you have labelled your electronic document with your name e.g. Jane Smith CV. If you are applying for a number of jobs you might have saved each copy of your CV with a version number. Make sure you take this off — you do not want the recruiter to see that you are working on version 32.

☑ If you put a date on your CV e.g. 28/11/15 it is instantly out of date the next day so if you want to put a date (not really necessary) put the year.

☑ Number the pages and length of document as a footer along with your name, e.g. Jane Smith, page 1 of 4. This will ensure that if someone has made a mistake in printing out the CVs, they will know that your CV is 4 pages long.

Font style and justification

Ideally the font size should be 11 (12 max) points and the font style Arial (or similar "sans serif" styles). Research suggests that Arial is the easiest font to read. Many academics use justified Times New Roman for document preparation but this can give very uneven spacing and therefore make it more difficult to read. See example below:

Arial, unjustified right margin

The purpose of a CV is to get you to an interview. CVs should be organic, highly flexible documents, which should be changed and adapted to every job you are applying for. A generic CV, which has not been adapted to the particulars of a job description, can be identified very easily and will be rejected.

Arial, justified right margin

The purpose of a CV is to get you to an interview. CVs should be organic, highly flexible documents, which should be changed and adapted to every job you are applying for. A generic CV, which has not been adapted to the particulars of a job description, can be identified very easily and will be rejected.

Times Roman, unjustified right margin

The purpose of a CV is to get you to an interview. CVs should be organic, highly flexible documents, which should be changed and adapted to every job you are applying for. A generic CV, which has not been adapted to the particulars of a job description, can be identified very easily and will be rejected.

Times Roman, justified right margin

The purpose of a CV is to get you to an interview. CVs should be organic, highly flexible documents, which should be changed and adapted to every job you are applying for. A generic CV, which has not been adapted to the particulars of a job description, can be identified very easily and will be rejected.

Bold, capitals, italics and underlining

Given the 20 second rule, the really important information needs to stand out, but if you have overused bold, capital letters, italics or underlining it is very difficult to read. Don't be tempted to use bold for the odd word- **it** just looks **strange**! WRITING IN CAPITAL LETTERS IS DIFFICULT TO READ and <u>underlined can be missed</u> if the document is photocopied several times. *Italics* can sometimes be much harder to read. <u>***NEVER DO ALL FOUR***</u>. Use bold only for headings and for authorship in papers (your name in bold!).

Bullet points

- Recruiters will not have the time to read long dense paragraphs.
- Using bullet points makes the text much quicker to read.
- Ensure the points are short, not sentences with a dot in front of them.

* What needs to change with your CV format?

General content

Write your name at the top and centre of the page in a slightly bigger font size. Include your title or qualifications (either Dr Jane Smith or Jane Smith PhD/DPhil). There is no need to write CV or curriculum vitae at the top of the page — it's obvious that this document is your CV.

For contact information use what works for you — a personal mobile is better than a shared office land line. A contact email address can be your work email address. Don't give the recruiter too many options — which should they ring/email? If you put links to webpages ensure they are up to date (and relevant).

There is no need to have an address on your CV. Don't be tempted to put your work address as your contact address. Although you may feel that you spend most of your life at work, you don't actually live there and when you are applying for a job, you are doing so as a private citizen, not a representative of your institution. Under no circumstances use the department's headed notepaper. If you do feel the need for an address, put your home address at the end. There is no need for it to take up valuable space on the first page. If you work with animals, we would strongly advise that you do not put your home address on your CV. If you send out your CV to an agency you do not want your home address to be seen as you cannot control where the agency will send it.

In the UK it is unlawful to discriminate against anyone in terms of their age, sex, marital status, disability, race, religion and belief, gender reassignment, pregnancy and maternity, or sexual orientation. Therefore, this information does not need to go on your CV. You may be asked to fill in a "monitoring form" with your application but these are detached by HR before your application proceeds.

When people talk about career breaks, they generally are speaking about time off due to illness or family needs (maternity/paternity/family illness/being a carer/parental leave). Unless specifically asked to include this in the application process, you do not have to give this information but if there are obvious career breaks, you may need to explain them, e.g. No publications in 2013? Put a *next to the date and say "maternity leave" if that is the reason for the break.

Some additional points are on the check list below to ensure your CV is a winner!

☐ Write "Qualifications" (not "Education").
☐ In your qualifications list, only include higher education i.e. degree and beyond (things that give you letters after your name) together with date awarded unless you need to demonstrate something (language qualifications for instance).
☐ Do not over-label the CV — don't waste space. e.g. *"Email address*: xxxx".
☐ Include the title of your PhD research project.

☐ Have "Employment" not "Work experience".

☐ Emphasise your key job duties.

☐ Use a clear reverse chronological order to your career history — most recent first.

☐ If you have to fill in an application form you may still be able to submit a CV, and you may find that doing the CV helps you fill in the application form.

☐ Emphasise the last 5 years (apart from qualifications).

☐ Use strong words to describe achievements, e.g. excellent, driven, expert, committed, focussed (not: competent, hope, expect....).

☐ Do not list outside interests such as reading, skiing, knitting (unless exceptional or relevant).

☐ Avoid using humour — it's a professional document and people have different senses of humour.

Academic CVs

Qualifications

Most academic CVs will start with a section on qualifications. As a postdoc this section should be entitled qualifications (professional degrees) rather than education (what happened at school). Unless requested to do so, only list your post-school qualifications i.e. first degree, masters, PhD. Do keep a record of your school qualifications, you may need them at some point. You will need to include a date for your qualifications but this can be year rather than day, month and year.

For some the award date of a PhD is quite different to the *viva* date, submission date, or graduation date. Our advice is that you use the date on your PhD certificate. In the qualifications section you need to include your thesis title in *italics*. It is not necessary to include your undergraduate dissertation unless specifically requested to do so. You do not need to write "thesis title" as it will be obvious.

Employment

The next section should be "employment" — not "work experience" (British context: something you do for a couple of weeks whilst at school). For a 2–3 page CV (excluding publications), about a third of page one of your CV needs to be a description of what you are currently doing. Use bullet points, not prose, to describe your current role and responsibilities. Make sure that what you are listing corresponds with the requirements of the post that you are applying for and list them in order of importance. Do not just echo your job description here — give a sense of what you, the talented postdoc that you are, actually do! A simple job description could be given by pretty much every other postdoc applying — the employer needs to know why YOU?

After your current post, list your previous employment but be careful that this does not end up being a long list of very short term work. The emphasis should be on what you have done during the past 5 years. If you did a 3-month internship 10 years ago, this should not be on your CV. A CV is a summary of the *relevant* skills, experience and qualifications for the role you are seeking to secure.

The rest of it!

If you have been awarded a prize or a grant and this is relevant to what you are applying for, put this on the first page.

What you are applying for will dictate the sequence of the remaining sections. If you are applying for a lectureship, you will need a section on the teaching that you have done. Under teaching put the course (no need for the code) level, type of teaching and whether you received any feedback. Also, be descriptive in your role. Tutorials for first year undergraduate biochemistry students can mean that you delivered pre-prepared material or that you designed, delivered, evaluated and re-designed a series of tutorials (both valuable but quite different experiences).

Publication lists are usually at the end and have no limit on pages! Authorship of papers should start on a separate page with the header "Publications". It is important to highlight your authorship and the best way to see this is to put your name in bold. Number your publications if there are more than 10 and present the most recent first. You can include submitted work but "in prep" is too vague.

Should you include a section on outside interests? In academia, other academics are generally not interested in an applicant's outside interests. They want to see the papers the applicant has written, the research and fellowships/grants which have been awarded not what they do at the weekend.

Have you included:

- ☑ A "prizes and awards" section.
- ☑ A "grants and funding" section (even small grants count).
- ☑ Any outreach activities.
- ☑ Any further contribution to your discipline (committees, society memberships).
- ☑ Skills relevant to the job such as teaching, collaborative working, grant writing, conference presentations, technical skills, computer skills (providing beyond the Microsoft Word level!).

CVs for other roles

The classic academic CV is not suitable for the majority of roles outside higher education (HE). If writing a CV for a non-academic role, start from a blank piece of paper and build a CV appropriate to the role using the "Lego brick" method. If you are trying to move out of academia, you do not want your CV to look academic. Do have a hunt for example CVs for the industry you are applying to — they may look very different. You have a choice of the straightforward reverse chronological format or a more skills focused CV.

If you are transitioning to something completely different it can be helpful to write a mini statement at the top of your CV (under your name) explaining what you offer. If you were applying for a finance job for instance it might read "I am a talented data analyst and programmer who is experienced working with time dependent data. I am looking to apply these skills to the financial industry."

The straightforward reverse chronological formatting is more familiar but it would be best to start with your employment (or career history) and move the qualifications further down. Open with what you can do, not how "qualified" you are. Put yourself in the employer's shoes — do they want a postdoc who cannot get another academic position or someone who has the skills they need in abundance? You will need to emphasise skills and experiences alongside each role relevant to the application. For instance, under your current postdoc role you could highlight "management skills developed by guiding students and technicians." Other sections will depend on matching the role description in the advert. Unless they have asked for a list of publications (some roles might be interested in this) do not include them but highlight the number/quality in your communication skills.

A skills based CV answers the role description directly by leading with the relevant skills outlined by the recruiter. This format would highlight several of the key skills — providing evidence for each from across your range of experience. Each skill should have a couple of examples of you demonstrating this skill. The examples can be drawn from all your roles (employment, student years, voluntary or sporting). A short chronology of your work and qualifications can follow this section. Here is an example of the formatting (taken from someone seeking an administration role). A top tip is to use a table to keep everything lined up.

Jo Bloggs

07777 999999 jbloggs@gmail.com

I am an experienced, conscientious administrator whose thoughtful and people focused attitude has delivered excellent customer service. I bring organisation and attention to detail to roles and particularly enjoy working as a team member.

Key skills

Communication skills

I am at ease working with a wide range of people where I have a natural rapport. My reception experience demonstrated an open, approachable and friendly approach. My current role for Going Places Travel involves successful communication with both the public and other staff - who often defer more difficult transactions to me. As PTA social secretary (a post I held for 12 years) I had to communicate with parents and staff verbally and through advertising to ensure successful fundraising events.

Administration skills

I have developed my office skills through out my career and have held roles as a typist, receptionist, secretary, deputising for a PA and a more general administrator. I am adept at adapting to a new environment and have worked with a variety of computer systems. I have a strong, natural organisation skills and bring this to the workplace.

Customer service

I enjoy customer facing roles where my excellent people skills have been valued throughout my career. In my current role, I enjoy solving customers problems bring a common sense approach and a friendly attitude. Whilst working for London Care Services, providing lunchtime support for elderly people, I often went the extra mile to sit, talk and connect with those in my care.

Attention to detail

I pride myself in delivering a good job and throughout my career people have noted my attention to detail. I strive to understand what is expected of a role and then deliver to a high standard.

Employment history

2006 - present

Reservations Assistant, Going Places Travel
Direct customer service role providing coach travel solutions. Now an experienced member of the team providing support to colleagues.

An example of a skills based CV

Whichever format you choose you need to bear in mind that your academic experience may need translating — not everyone understands the context. Other sections might include training and development qualifications (software, technical skills). For some jobs such as medical writing, industry, a section on outside interests may be relevant.

Conclusion

The CV is a door opener — it gets you to the interview. You never get a second chance to make a first impression so it is well worth investing time and effort into the process. If you want to be invited to interview your chances of being invited are greatly increased by writing a CV specifically adapted to the role you are applying for. Remember to ask yourself "Why am I telling them this?"

Finally, your CV is probably one of the most important career documents that you will ever have so, keep it updated and fresh. Let it positively reflect all your skills, experience and expertise which will make you extremely employable.

What every postdoc needs to know about ... winning CVs

☑ Layout and design are important.
☑ Only include relevant experience and skills.
☑ Do research on the norms for CVs for the sector you are applying to.

Resources

Some good advice and example CVs at Monster Jobs, available at http://career-advice.monster.co.uk/cvs-applications/cv-advice/jobs.aspx
10 CV tips from jobs.ac.uk, available at http://www.jobs.ac.uk/careers-advice/cv-templates/1905/top-10-tips-for-writing-your-cv
Newspapers also offer CV advice alongside their jobs pages such as The Guardian, available at http://www.theguardian.com/careers/cv

Chapter 19

Interviews and Questions

Introduction

Congratulations on getting to interview! This means you have made it through the first round of selection but now is the time to accelerate with the preparation to ensure that you are fully prepared. Many interviews are short, and may feel rushed and stressful. In order to reduce stress (although a little bit of adrenaline can be helpful) you'll need to prepare. In this chapter we will give advice on preparing for interviews, some common mistakes, and some examples of interview questions.

Overview

Always bear in mind that every interviewer is trying to evaluate you on three criteria:

1. Are you able to do the job?
2. Are you willing to put in the effort to make the job a success?
3. Are you a good fit with the team/the company/the institution?

An ill prepared candidate will likely irritate the panel — and not get the job! You do not want to be remembered for the wrong reasons:

☒ Inability to answer simple questions e.g. why should we give the job to you?

⊠ Inappropriate clothes — never dress down for an interview; try and find out what the norms are and dress a bit smarter.
⊠ Being late.
⊠ Ignoring the guidelines.
⊠ Ignoring certain panel members — do not assume the only female and/or youngest person in the room is the most junior/ least significant.
⊠ Giving answers which are too long or too short.

Sadly, there is not enough space in this book to have a chapter on "Horrible interviews we have been part of." But the decisions and assessment the panel makes occur immediately as you walk into the room so even your entrance will be assessed, if only sub-consciously. Indeed, the impression you make at the reception desk, whilst not part of the formal interview or judgement, may make a difference. If a panel member is chatting with the receptionist who asks, "Have you made a decision about the candidates interviewed earlier?" and they say "We are still thinking about it; there are a couple of candidates we can't choose between. What were your first impressions?" The receptionist's opinion on someone being polite or friendly might tip things in your favour. The key thing to remember is that you need to approach the interview with the confidence and belief that you are the best person for the job and that you are a good fit with the organisation. In other words — you need to prepare, do a lot of background research, and demonstrate how you are the best candidate and therefore a perfect fit.

One way to prepare is to organise a mock interview. It may be that your institution's careers service or similar can offer this. If not, then ask someone you trust to help you run through some questions. Try to make the mock interview as realistic as possible; with them inviting you into the room, firing the questions at you, and then make time for feedback at the end.

Starting off at the interview

There are a few things to consider before you even start talking!

What to wear

Although most panels will not reject you because you are wearing the wrong clothes, they will judge you on it even if they are unaware of doing so. When panels are interviewing a lot of candidates (over 10) on one day it is often difficult by interview number seven to differentiate between candidates. So, panels will identify a "tag". For example, the candidate who is currently working at x, the candidate who has specialised in y. These "tags" are in relation to the experience the candidate has and what impact the candidate has on the panel. If you wear the wrong clothes for the interview your "tag" will be what you wore e.g. the one who wore jeans, the one who wore The bright yellow trousers. These are not good tags.

Some invitation to interview letters state what should be worn e.g. Royal Society University Research Fellowship invitations state, "wear business attire." It is much better to be "over smart" than too casual. If at this point you are thinking — "My research will speak for itself and I can wear what I like..." What the panel may perceive is that you don't respect the process, them, or what they represent. Don't take this risk. The panel are not just assessing you on your suitability for the role but also you as a future colleague and how easy you will be to work with.

Even if your day-to-day research business is conducted in jeans and a t-shirt, for an interview it needs to be more formal. Ideally you are aiming to look 20% smarter than your interviewers showing that you respect the rules of engagement here. Men should wear a suit or smart jacket and we would advise a tie. Women, as is always the way, have more choice but should wear a suit or smart dress. These options let you dress down i.e. you can remove the tie or jacket if need be but jeans give you no way to smarten up. The authors have also learnt from bitter experience not to wear brand new shoes to an interview.

Location, location, location

Make sure you know the location of the interview and arrive with plenty of time to spare. If possible, do a "dry run" to get there.

Assume trains/buses will be running late that day! You may also have to sign in, get a security pass or park any luggage somewhere. Try to walk into the interview just holding what you need, ready to go — divesting yourself of coat and bags eats into your interview time and looks clumsy.

Shaking hands

It can feel very awkward if you get this wrong. Shaking hands is culturally driven, and will depend on the Chair of the panel (the person in charge), the set up of the interview room and the other panel members. Our advice is to take the lead from the Chair of the panel. If he or she puts their hand out, then shake it. If, when you walk into the interview room the panel stand up and approach you with their hands out then shake them. (You may want to practice if you are unaccustomed to shaking hands; "limp lily" or "bonecrusher" are not the "tag" that you want!) If the panel are all sitting, it can feel very awkward for both candidate and panel members if you attempt to go around the room shaking everyone's hands. Some interview rooms are so small that it is not possible for the panel members to move from their seats, so then what ensues is awkward stretching across a table or a panel member just waving at you. Just take the lead from the Chair.

Types of interview

There are a wide range of types of interview and our best advice is to assume you are being assessed in some way, even informally, as soon as you step onto the campus or site. Interviews can be made up of the following components:

- ☐ The standard face-to-face questioning, either with a couple of people or a panel (it is ok to ask who will be interviewing you but they don't have to tell you!).
- ☐ A presentation to your interview panel.

Avoid the limp lily or bonecrusher handshakes — practice!

- ☐ A presentation to a wider audience (check who your audience will be so that you can adjust the content accordingly).
- ☐ All candidates giving a presentation and watching each other's presentations as part of the audience.
- ☐ Group tasks where they are looking for initiative, team work, leadership.
- ☐ Assessment centres including psychometric tools.
- ☐ A tour of the facilities.
- ☐ A meal with the team/management.
- ☐ A test of skills (an inbox exercise or an assessed task).
- ☐ A video call interview (think about the background behind you!).
- ☐ A phone interview (stand up to sound more confident).
- ☐ A series of interviews with different people throughout the day.
- ☐ A series of interview rounds (initial, second round).

Try to find out as much as possible before the day and do let the panel know if you require anything adapting (e.g. if you are unable to complete a walking tour, have dietary constraints or hearing difficulties). However, do not try to bargain with the panel on the start time of the interview (if you can't get there for 9 am how would you get to work?). If it's an early morning start go the night before and have a walk around the campus/town.

Presentations

Many interviews (particularly in academia) include a presentation as part of the interview. This key part of the process is usually delivered at the start of the interview. An ill prepared presentation can ruin a candidate's chances of being appointed and yet, from our experience of interviews, many presentations are either poorly prepared, overly complicated or haven't followed the guidelines the candidates have been given. Some golden rules:

Stick to time

If the interview includes a 10 mins presentation aim to talk for 9 mins. Most presenters, when they relax into giving a talk tend to add more than they had initially planned which leads to the danger of overrunning. A panel will not give you extra points for overrunning and in general will be irritated or stop you short.

Practice

Practice the talk, preferably in front of someone, so that you give a polished presentation. Ask for honest, constructive feedback and then use it to make the presentation better. Repeat the process, if necessary. Think about the adage, "Tell them what you are going to tell them, tell them it, and then tell them what you have told them" i.e. make sure your audience absolutely know your key point at the end of the 10 mins. If you have the opportunity to give presentations in your research team or department then seize them. Not only will you get valuable feedback on your research, you will gain confidence in dealing with questions, and practice will help you to improve your style of delivery.

Tailor to the audience

If you have been asked to give a sample lecture to a group of first year undergraduates, then make sure that you adjust the content accordingly. Similarly, if you are asked to give a presentation about your research, the content for a faculty-wide seminar may be significantly different to what you would include for the research team or department you are hoping to join. If you are asked to present how you would tackle a part of the new role then try to highlight your previous experience, whilst translating it to the audience.

Visual aids

If the interview letter says "you may send your slides in advance," send the slides in advance because this will save time at the interview. Take back-ups: print outs, a pdf version, saved on a USB data stick and emailed to yourself — whatever you think most useful. Some points to consider:

- ☑ Be prepared, if necessary, to give the talk without visual aids.
- ☑ Check you know how to move between slides.
- ☑ Don't include fancy (some would say irritating) animations for no reason.
- ☑ Be cautious about the inclusion of videos or relying on an internet connection (including the use of Prezi).

If you know the size and format of the room you will be presenting in, there may be an opportunity to bring samples or models to hand round.

> To use PowerPoint (or Keynote/Prezi...) or not?
>
> Some interviews specifically say that PowerPoint will not be available, others say you may use PowerPoint if you wish. Before automatically deciding to use PowerPoint ask yourself these questions:
>
> - Does PowerPoint enhance my presentation?
> - Does it add anything?
> - If the projector broke down would I be able to convey the main message of my talk?
> - Have I spent more time on fancy graphics and simulations than the content?
> - Am I confident enough to use PowerPoint without needing to check the slides (and if I am do I therefore need the slides?)

Interview questions

Most of the interview will be controlled by questions. You can be prepared for the type of questions to expect by doing research on the interviewer, the department/institute/company and the type of position for which you are being interviewed. However, no interview is so completely structured that you can plan it totally in advance.

What if you can't answer a question? Your mind goes blank, you don't understand what they have asked, or they have asked so many questions in one that you don't know where to start? These are all common in the interview setting. So, the first thing to try and remember is don't panic. It's OK to pause briefly to think before answering and if you don't understand a question do ask for clarification. You can say, "I think what you are asking is ..." or "I think there are several questions there, I will tackle the one on ... first."

What follows are some example questions asked by interviewers. They have been grouped under various themes but obviously one question could be appropriate to several themes. In the interview it is rare that set themes are pursued, but rather the interviewers move between questions to test your suitability for the job. We have provided some guidance for that type of question and then listed other questions you may be asked. We have limited our lists to 10! You will find many lists of questions if you search. Just as you revised for exams, keep practicing with new questions.

The panel are looking for specific, intelligent and well thought out examples from your past experience, that highlight your skills, strengths and expertise. It is essential to prepare solid, specific examples to use in your interview. For example, it is not enough to say that you demonstrate research leadership every day, you must go into enough detail to say, for example, "during this project XYZ when my PI was away and there was no one else in the lab and a PhD student needed some information urgently, I took the initiative to find out the students exact requirements and found the information in the project files, and checked with another researcher that it was ok to distribute this information. The result in the end was that the student's project was not held up and ended up not missing their deadline, and my PI was very impressed with the initiative I had demonstrated...." Talk from your experience rather than the hypothetical future — we can all be perfect hypothetically!

Some common questions with answers

Why do you want to work here?

To answer this question, you must have researched the department/company you are applying to. Reply with the organisation's attributes as you see them and say how you would contribute to their success.

How do you feel about your progress to date?

This question is not geared solely to rate your progress; it also rates your self-esteem and your awareness of your progress in relation to your peers (remember it is a competition). Be positive with specific examples. If you have had a set back and it's clear on your CV, address it briefly, and state what you learnt (positively). If you are interviewing for a role outside your current arena, paint a picture of how your experience is useful.

What would you like to be doing 5 years from now?

Make your answer ambitious but realistic. If the questions are being asked at a lectureship interview, it is unlikely that you will be a professor in 5 years' time so you need to focus on your ambitions for your research, your group and the development of your students. Find out what others do 5 years down the line from joining there.

What are your biggest accomplishments?

Keep your answers job-related. Give an honest answer and a specific example.

Tell me about yourself.

This is not an invitation to ramble on. If the context isn't clear, you need to know more about the questions before giving an answer. Whichever direction your answer ultimately takes be sure that it has some relevance to the job you are applying for. For example, if the job includes a lot of travel and you enjoy travelling, you may want to use that as information about yourself.

How well do you feel other people rated your job performance?

This is quite a challenging question and again you need to give a straight, honest but sensible answer. You might use examples from an appraisal or a development course you have attended which included a 360 degree evaluation and feedback.

What is your greatest strength?

Isolate high points from your background and build in a couple of your key personal qualities, such as pride in your work, reliability and the ability to stick with a difficult task, yet change course rapidly when required.

What is your greatest weakness?

This is a direct invitation to put your head in a noose. Decline the invitation. If there is a minor part of the job at hand where you lack knowledge — but knowledge you will obviously pick up quickly — use that. For instance: "I haven't worked with this type of spreadsheet before but, given my experience with six other types, I should be able to pick it up in a few days." Another option is to design the answer so your weakness is ultimately a positive characteristic. For example: "I always give each project my best shot, so if I sometimes feel others aren't pulling their weight, I find it a little frustrating. I try to overcome it with a positive attitude that I hope will catch on." Also consider the technique of putting a problem in the past and showing how you overcame it.

What are you looking for in your next job?

Avoid saying what you want the employer to give you; you must say what you want in terms of what you can give to the employer. The key word is "contribution".

Why do you want to leave your current job? Or Why did you leave your last job?

You should have an acceptable reason for leaving every job you have held but if you don't, pick one of the six acceptable reasons from this employment industry "CLAMPS" formula:

- *Challenge:* you weren't able to grow professionally.
- *Location:* the journey to work was unreasonably long.
- *Advancement:* there was nowhere for you to go.
- *Money:* you were underpaid for your skills and contribution.
- *Pride and prestige:* you wanted to be with a better company.
- *Security:* the company was not stable.

Can I contact your previous line manager for a reference? Why not?

If you have had a poor relationship with your manager, then you need to answer this very carefully. Do not wade into a long description of all the arguments you had with them. If you have chosen other referees, then explain why they will be more helpful to this potential employer. You can always ask them to delay asking for a reference until you are offered the job stating the reason of not wanting to take up your manager's time unless necessary.

Research

These questions are aimed at testing your research ideas and ambitions, whether you are the right person and if you are aware of the wider context of the significance of your research for your group, department and university e.g. the Research Excellence Framework (REF). You must demonstrate awareness of current trends in the field, impact, ethical considerations as well as your personal progress and standing. Even a non-academic job might ask about your research. Ensure you pitch your explanation at the right level.

1. What makes your proposed research world leading?
2. How would you describe your proposed research to a 10-year-old?
3. Outline your research interests and how you see them developing over the next three to 5 years.
4. Which of your publications would you submit to the REF and why?
5. Where would you apply for funding for your research?
6. What is the societal impact of your research?
7. What are the potential risks involved in this project, and how will you deal with them if things go wrong?
8. How does your work complement existing work in the department?

9. Would you foresee collaborations with others in the institution (outside of the department)?
10. You are now moving from being told what to do to telling other people what to do. How would you run a research group?

Teaching

These questions are aimed at testing your teaching knowledge and ideas and whether you fully understand what it is to be a lecturer (which is quite a different role to being a researcher). See Chapters 7 and 17. The panel will expect you to have done some background work on what is already taught in the department and be able to describe how you can add to what they currently teach or supplement the current provision. You may be asked about teaching/training in non-academic jobs. Be prepared to explain your experience clearly.

1. Why do you want to become a lecturer?
2. What ideas do you have about developing an MSc course and how would you go about it?
3. What experience do you have of course development and what was your contribution?
4. What aspects of *<insert appropriate tutorial subject>* do you think students will struggle with?
5. Teaching and learning — are they the same thing?
6. How would you change/improve the teaching we offer?
7. How do you make sure that the weaker students are following your course?
8. How do you adapt your teaching style for large groups of students?
9. What experience do you have of supervising students — either undergraduate or postgraduate?
10. Would you agree to teach modules that are outside your comfort zone and if yes how long do you need for preparation?

General questions

These questions are much more likely to be asked in interviews outside academia. Some of the questions are aimed at you demonstrating that you understand different types of working environments and cultures and that you have the skills to reflect on what you are good at, what you need to work on and how you can ensure you keep developing.

1. Tell me about your current and previous bosses: what kind of people are they?
2. What are the most satisfying, and the most frustrating aspects of your present job?
3. Describe a time when you felt ineffective: what did you do about it and what was the outcome?
4. Can you describe, in the same way, a time when you felt particularly effective?
5. Were your assignments handled individually or were they a team effort?
6. What are the most important factors you require in a job: how should it be structured to provide you with satisfaction?
7. What is the biggest problem at work you have had to overcome?
8. Looking back over your career to date, which job would you change given your current direction?
9. If you had total executive control what one thing would you change?
10. Whom do you find it difficult to work with?

Professional activities

These questions are aimed at testing whether you would be willing to do work which contributes to the department outside your teaching and research duties or might reflect a commitment using related skills (for instance writing newsletter pieces for a worthy cause if you are going for a writing job). Sometimes referred to as "citizenship". Remember that a lectureship role is roughly divided in to teaching, research and administration. These examples may be very useful in other contexts.

1. What contribution do you make to your current organisation?
2. What makes a successful seminar?
3. When you are involved in organising a conference, what is your contribution to the team and the activity?
4. When refereeing papers, what do you look for?
5. What involvement do you have with your professional body?
6. What learned society are you in?
7. What do you contribute to your discipline?
8. How do you work to make society better?
9. How do you bring people together in your current organisation?
10. How do you encourage people into your field?

Challenging questions

Sometimes you get questions which are far from encouraging and you will be tempted to ask yourself *"Well, why am I being interviewed?"* These questions need honest answers but keep the tone upbeat. Avoid the temptation to bad mouth people or be overly defensive. Remember, sometimes your CV has been included on the short list when you do not completely match the person specification.

1. Why have you changed/stayed in jobs so frequently/long?
2. Why is your salary so low given these achievements in your CV?
3. Why were you made redundant?
4. Why have you been out of work for so long?
5. What difficulties or failures are pushing you out of your present job?
6. What sorts of things do you delegate?
7. Have you ever had a bad experience with an employer?
8. Give an example of a time when you handled a major crisis.
9. What motivates you?
10. Why is there a gap in your employment history?

Potential

The better interviewer will avoid hypothetical questions except where he or she is trying to assess your suitability not just for the job on offer but a career with the organisation. Ensure your answers are based on solid research about the field and the environment and are realistically achievable.

1. What do you see as the next step in your career?
2. How ambitious are you?
3. In the long-term what do you want to achieve?
4. How does this job fit in with your career aspirations?
5. What do you see yourself doing in 5/10 years' time?
6. What do you think you can do for us?
7. What is the ideal job for you?
8. What goals would you have in mind if you got this role?
9. What are you looking for in terms of career development?
10. Do you see yourself offering leadership in this field?

Achievement questions

These questions will provide an opportunity to express your achievements. This is no time to be modest, just don't over do it! If you can use figures to help illustrate the achievement and make sure you put it into context (not everyone will understand how amazing three *Nature* papers are!) Remember that questions are best answered in the light of the job you are aiming for so ensure your successes link to the job description.

1. What are you doing best right now?
2. What is your greatest achievement to date?
3. What did you achieve in that job?
4. How did you change the job?
5. What are your current job targets?
6. For what will you be remembered for in that job?
7. Why do you think you got that job?

8. What was it in your performance that made you a candidate for promotion?
9. What are you most proud of in your career?
10. What makes you feel you did a good job?

Competency based questions

These questions need you to use evidence. Be specific and truthful. Avoid naming people — use the terms "colleague" or "student". Again try to align your answer to the job in hand.

1. Tell me about a time when you had to deal with a difficult situation.
2. Give me an example of when you have gone above and beyond the call of duty.
3. Give me an example of when you have really impressed a colleague.
4. Give me an example of when you have solved a problem.
5. Give me an example of when you have showed your initiative.
6. Give me an example of when you have had to deal with a difficult colleague and what you did.
7. What is the best feedback you have received?
8. What is the worst feedback you have been given?
9. Give examples of ideas you've had or implemented.
10. Tell me about a time where you had to deal with conflict on the job.

General questions

There will always be questions that don't fit into a category — and here they are! If you are prepared for most of the obvious questions you should be able to handle the odd curveball question.

1. Why do you want to work here?
2. What attracts you to the organisation?
3. What can you bring to the role?

4. Where can you add value?
5. Why should we employ you?
6. Can you provide me with examples of your past experiences and achievements?
7. How do you organise yourself?
8. What are three positive things your last boss would say about you?
9. What do you know about the company? How did you find that out?
10. How would your colleagues describe you in three words?

Questions for you to ask at the end of the interview

Normally at the end of an interview, the chair of the panel will ask you if you have any questions. This is not the time to produce a list of 20 questions ranging from salary to child care provision! If you feel you should ask a question, make sure it's a question which you could not have found out the answer to e.g. "What is the institute's 5-year strategy?" — this is likely to be available on the website. A common question is "When will you be letting candidates know?" If this has already been answered don't waste the opportunity by saying "I don't have any questions" instead have a positive concise closing statement or remark to end the interview on.

Conclusion

Interviews are stressful processes and you need to prepare. Ideally you want to walk in the room feeling confident and assured and that you have done everything you could do to be an excellent candidate. However, interviews are a competition, there is normally only one position and even if you have done all the preparation you could, you may not be successful and another candidate may just have more experience, expertise, is a better fit. Not getting the job doesn't necessarily mean you couldn't have done it, it's just that the other candidate was judged as being able to do it better. After the initial disappointment do request feedback. If you say

"Can I have some feedback?" you are likely to receive a bland response e.g. "We enjoyed meeting you but the successful candidate was a more suitable fit." There is not much you can work on with this feedback so a much better question is "What would I have needed to do to be offered the job?" With this question you are more likely to receive more constructive feedback.

Best of luck!

What every postdoc needs to know about ... interviews

- ☑ Preparation is vital.
- ☑ Have a mock interview.
- ☑ Be positive!

Resources

Tips from The Guardian (nearby pages also good), available at http://www.theguardian.com/careers/2015/dec/30/the-best-job-interview-tips-of-2015

Some good advice from Forbes (the business magazine), available at http://www.forbes.com/sites/jacquelynsmith/2013/01/11/how-to-ace-the-50-most-common-interview-questions/#4ca220c44873

Chapter 20

Conclusions: What Do We Hope You Know Now?

In summary this book boils down to one simple rule:

A postdoc is not a career

We have given you a guide to the beginning, middle and end of the postdoc story but your personal career story will go on from the postdoc years. There will be a time when you can look back! Our hope is that with this book, ownership of your own career, a determination to get the best from things, and a big bucket of coffee (from one of the authors) the process of looking back will raise a smile.

The authors have learnt much from writing this book together — processes, communication and an insight into the world of publishing. It was something new and challenging but then that is what life is about. So, relish the postdoc as it offers so much development, friendships and a myriad of potential exciting futures.

What every postdoc needs to know about ... our wishes for you

- ☑ Postdocs are the most amazing and talented bunch of people.
- ☑ We love working with you.
- ☑ We wish you all the best for your future career.

The authors are happy to be contacted in the following ways:

Dr Liz Elvidge at e.elvidge@imperial.ac.uk.
Dr Carol Spencely via rdp@surrey.ac.uk.
Dr Emma Williams via Twitter @ejwsolutions.

Chapter 21

Over to You

Maybe it is our scientific background but we do like lists. Our development background demands that participants set actions. So this last chapter is a summary with calls to action! Don't forget to set your actions as specific, measurable, achievable, realistic and time bound (SMART). Good luck!

Here's what every postdoc needs to know. What actions will you take?

Choosing a postdoc

- ☑ It should be an active and considered decision.
- ☑ Use your research skills to consider the people, project and place.
- ☑ A postdoc is not a career but a step to the next thing.

* Action:

The UK higher education scene

- ☑ Research continues to be a strong part within the UK's long tradition of Higher Education, which is a sector that is constantly evolving and changing.
- ☑ Support and development opportunities for postdocs within the UK higher education institutes (HEIs) are varied and form part of the institutions' strategies to attract and retain great researchers

(who will carry out great research that is associated with their institution). Find out what is on offer at places you plan to apply to.

☑ All employers differ, HEIs in the UK are included in this. Oxford is very different to Cambridge (which they are at constant lengths to prove, not least by the annual boat race on the Thames), and these institutions differ dramatically to Imperial, Surrey and Liverpool. The point being that your postdoc experience will be shaped by the place you choose to do it, so it is worth investigating the options.

* Action:

Coming to the UK

☑ Use your research skills to find out as much as you can about the UK.
☑ Embrace opportunities to explore new places and meet new people.
☑ Do not blame us for the weather!

* Action:

Getting the most out of your time as postdoc

☑ Know why you are doing a postdoc and what you would like to get out of the time.
☑ Take advantage of any opportunities for training, development, sitting on committees, entrepreneurial schemes, teaching, mentoring ….
☑ Try things out and explore options to help you succeed in your career plans.

* Action:

The relationship with your Principal Investigator (PI)

☑ Communicate early and often.
☑ Do not assume the quality of your work will speak for itself, be professional.
☑ The relationship is important. Make it work for you.

* Action:

Publishing

☑ It's important; so, have a plan and put it into action.
☑ Feedback is essential.
☑ Understand the system you are working including bibliometrics and altmetrics.

* Action:

Teaching and supervision

☑ Teaching develops a range of skills useful in your current role and any future job.
☑ Think broadly and widely about the range of opportunities available to teach within your institution and beyond.
☑ Consider participating in courses and qualifications offered by your institution that are designed to enhance your understanding of teaching and educational theory and practice.

* Action:

Transferable skills development and taking opportunities

☑ Transferable skills are skills that you can use in multiple settings/roles (and not just something made up by trainers/ staff development managers).
☑ Transferable skills are often undervalued, under-appreciated and called "soft" (not complimentary in a tough working environment). They are considered to be "obvious" or "nothing special" by postdocs and academics … they are not. This is completely wrong. They are integral to your current role and permeate through all you do (even if that is invisibly). It is vital that they are made visible for securing a future job.
☑ Find out what skills you have, what skills you need, and what skills you want to develop.

✳ Action:

Networking

☑ Ask yourself what do you need to know and who knows it.
☑ Always have a business card with you.
☑ Thank everyone, for everything.

✳ Action:

Risk and reward

☑ If we could predict the outcomes with certainty, there would be no need to do the research in the first place!
☑ Unexpected results or failures can, on occasions, lead to unexpected positive outcomes.
☑ Get creative in thinking what you can do with what you have rather than dwelling on what might have been.

✳ Action:

Increasing productivity and reducing stress

☑ Investigate and acknowledge the existence of Imposter Syndrome, if relevant.
☑ You do not have to be superman/woman.
☑ Ask for help and advice.

✳ Action:

Diversity in research

☑ There are many dimensions to the diverse research groups and academic teams you are likely to work in.
☑ We all have unconscious bias in the way we deal with people, acknowledging it and setting up ways to tackle it are key to overcoming these biases.
☑ There are laws, policies and initiatives to address some of the biases in the workplace.

* Action:

Research integrity and ethics

☑ Get familiar with your institution's rules on IP.
☑ Think about where you draw the boundaries in work relationships.
☑ Being a postdoc means you are now a research professional.

* Action:

Taking responsibility for your career and decision making

☑ Your career is your responsibility.
☑ Make a plan ... one that will be reviewed and changed, no doubt, but you will achieve more with one than without.
☑ Don't wait. Start planning from day one of your postdoc.

* Action:

Careers beyond academia

☑ There are lots of possibilities for people with your skill set — don't let that put you off.
☑ Develop a strategy for investigating options.
☑ Try not to let the expectations of others hijack your choices.

* Action:

Fellowships

☑ Springboard to an academic career.
☑ Get organised early.
☑ Ask for feedback and help at each stage.

* Action:

Getting a lectureship

☑ There is no automatic step from a postdoc to a lectureship.

☑ Assess the skills and experience required for lectureships and take action during your postdoc to gain these.

☑ When you have seen a lectureship advertised in your field, do background research on the type of university it is e.g. Research-intensive, teaching-led and assess whether you are a good fit.

✳ Action:

Winning CVs

☑ Layout and design are important.

☑ Only include relevant experience and skills.

☑ Do research on the norms for CVs for the sector you are applying to.

✳ Action:

Interviews

☑ Preparation is vital.

☑ Have a mock interview.

☑ Be positive!

Index